JUSTICE AND LOVE

JUSTICE AND LOVE

A Philosophical Dialogue

MARY ZOURNAZI AND ROWAN WILLIAMS

BLOOMSBURY ACADEMIC
LONDON • NEW YORK • OXFORD • NEW DELHI • SYDNEY

BLOOMSBURY ACADEMIC
Bloomsbury Publishing Plc
50 Bedford Square, London, WC1B 3DP, UK
1385 Broadway, New York, NY 10018, USA
29 Earlsfort Terrace, Dublin 2, Ireland

BLOOMSBURY, BLOOMSBURY ACADEMIC and the Diana logo are trademarks of
Bloomsbury Publishing Plc

First published in Great Britain 2021
Reprinted 2021 (four times)

Cover design by Charlotte Daniels
Cover image: *The Judgment of Solomon*, pen and ink (16th Century) by Bartolomeo Passarotti
(Photo © Bonhams London / Bridgeman Images)

Bloomsbury Publishing Plc does not have any control over, or responsibility for, any third-party websites
referred to or in this book. All internet addresses given in this book were correct at the time of going to
press. The author and publisher regret any inconvenience caused if addresses have changed or sites have
ceased to exist, but can accept no responsibility for any such changes.

A catalogue record for this book is available from the British Library.

Library of Congress Cataloging-in-Publication Data
Names: Zournazi, Mary, author. | Williams, Rowan, 1950– author.
Title: Justice and love : a philosophical debate / Mary Zournazi and Rowan Williams.
Description: London ; New York : Bloomsbury Academic, 2020. |
Includes bibliographical references and index.
Identifiers: LCCN 2020029950 | ISBN 9781350090378 (hb) | ISBN 9781350090361 (pb) |
ISBN 9781350090408 (epdf) | ISBN 9781350090385 (ebook)
Subjects: LCSH: Justice–Moral and ethical aspects. | Justice–Religious aspects. |
Love–Moral and ethical aspects. | Love–Religious aspects.
Classification: LCC BJ1533.J9 Z68 2020 | DDC 172/.2—dc23
LC record available at https://lccn.loc.gov/2020029950

ISBN: HB: 978-1-3500-9037-8
        PB: 978-1-3500-9036-1
        ePDF: 978-1-3500-9040-8
        eBook   978-1-3500-9038-5

Typeset by RefineCatch Limited, Bungay, Suffolk
Printed and bound in Great Britain

To find out more about our authors and books visit www.bloomsbury.com
and sign up for our newsletters.

In our era, the road to holiness necessarily passes through the world of action.
Dag Hammarskjöld

CONTENTS

CONVERSATIONS BETWEEN SOULS

Ben Okri

I am addicted to dialogues. The best of them are not just two people investigating a subject, spiralling round themes. The best dialogues are revelatory. With rigorous logic they investigate urgent questions at the heart of our lives.

The beauty of such a dialogue depends firstly on a sensitive and intelligent interlocutor and a central thinker who responds to questions with generosity and truthfulness. More than that, the central thinker ought to be one with whom we would like to engage in conversation about the great and the small things of life. The dialogue can be imaginary, as with some of Schopenhauer's dialogues about religion; or they can be real as in the poetic dialogues of Plato. In the case of the latter Socrates is the ideal person one would eternally like to engage in civilised conversation as one gets taken over the edge of one's perceptions.

Dialogues are the ideal way to probe, even tentatively, important subjects. It is not an accident that Plato was, among other things, a writer of plays. And a good philosophical dialogue has to also be a fine piece of dialogue making, of conversations between souls.

Rowan Williams is that rare being, a man of religion who can and will engage in the most serious contemplation of the questions of justice from a secular as well as a spiritual viewpoint. The measure of the man is in the depth of the interrogation, an unwillingness to settle for easy solutions, and the courage to accept that sometimes a problem can be dealt with first on a level of faith.

He is here in conversation with Mary Zournazi, an Australian writer and philosopher, author of 'Hope: new philosophies For Change.' She makes for an intelligent, responsive, and dare I say an intuitive interlocutor. Her questions are always thoughtful and her responses often surprising and intimate.

The beauty of these conversations, which took place over a number of years, is that they happen in the midst of world events that have ancient roots and that also continue to exercise and perplex us. This makes for the earthiness of the dialogues. They don't take place in an abstract academic space. They happen here, now, while the Syrian crisis spirals out of control; while right wing governments with their anti-democratic policies proliferate in the world; while Brexit continues to divide the populace; and extend even into edges of global concerns raised by the current pandemic. In many ways the background of world crisis gives not only a testamentary quality to these conversations but also lends them the sparks of the forge.

The difficulty of our times is how to bring thought to the heat of our contemporary crisis. These are times that call for great thinkers. These are times when it seems that thought has fallen asleep, where truth has been blurred out of existence, and when the myths that we live by have been distorted beyond recognition.

A post-truth world means that we spiral ever in the stasis of the relativities of interpretation. Reality – what happened – has never been more contested. It is harder now to think anything for sure, harder to be clear in one's conception and grasp of the world. Many things that sustained a clear reading of the world are falling away.

Reading declines even when information has never been more plentiful. Libraries in Essex have seen their book number drop by 470,000 in about 10 years. Long before corona virus the Internet made us self-isolators. Where there was community there is a prevalence of solipsism. And yet we have never needed one another more. The gap between the rich and the poor widens; the gap between the right and the left becomes more of a chasm; environmental catastrophe draws the apocalypse ever closer day by day, with our collusion and our silence.

An enlightened politics has never been more needed in the life of the planet, in the lives of people; and yet an enlightened politics, a politics of heart, has never been more absent from our times. Anyone who isn't conscious of the gravity of the conditions of the world is profoundly and dangerously asleep to the fury of contemporary life. We are on the edge of a precipice and even as you read these lines we are sliding over.

These times call for a new kind of urgency of thought. Central to that urgency of thought is the issue of justice. It is important that justice is also at the centre of these dialogues. For, on the whole, the culture has had a narrow idea of the possibilities of justice. We often bring too many binaries to the notion and reality of justice. We tend mostly to think that justice is for someone, a group, a race, a class, a gender. But justice is both more intimate and more cosmic than that. There is the justice of those who suffer, or who have suffering inflicted on them; but there is also the mysterious operation of justice on those who do the inflicting, the perpetrators. Beyond that obvious binary there is justice due to the earth. In short justice is a more complex idea than one might first think. In these dialogues it is linked to love, to beauty, to witnessing. It is at the very heart of the sanity or the survival of cultures and civilisations. Without love we will wilt and die, but without justice we will tear ourselves apart and perish. Justice is at the heart of the contemporary malaise and evil that is spreading throughout the world, both in political and environmental terms.

As with all true dialogues there is a spiralling round this most vexed and thorny of issues, a spiralling and a radiating inwards and outwards to unexpectedly related themes. The beauty of these dialogues is that they are underlined with the practical as well as the cultural. Literature and art, aesthetics and praxis, contemplation and activism, all have their place in the universe of these conversations.

A society is only as alive as its core conversations. The art of conversation is dying. This is a time of monologues, soliloquies, solipsistic speech in twitter-sphere. This is a time in which we talk from our solitudes, our loneliness; a time in which we are talked at. Politicians talk at us, not to us; certainly, rarely, with us. The newspapers, television, radio, Internet, all talk at us. When we come together to talk, we talk at one another.

Conversation, which is the highest spiritual respect that one soul can pay to another in the social sphere, requires attention and great listening. For if you don't listen, you can't truly respond. Listening requires, in a way, that the ego be silent; it ought to 'get thee behind me,' as Jesus said to Satan. To listen is to give space within oneself to the other, to open a stage within oneself for the other to perform their being; and for them to do the same for you, in response, in the soul's dance. In this way we truly begin to understand one another. And from this genuine understanding we can act properly, fairly, justly. In a sense there can be no true justice where there is no true listening. It is in conversation, in dialogue, that we rehearse the realities, the notions, the complexities of justice. Dialogue is the micro world of democracy.

The movement from the micro to the macro and back again characterises the nature of these dialogues. The micro world of the emotions, of the nature of learning, of the need for a high quality of attentiveness, for patience, the taking time to absorb the meaning of experience, allowing others time to revaluate their positions, the possibilities of learning from oneself whether one is right or wrong, an important aspect of conflict resolution, are seen as invaluable – even at the risk of sailing close to the terrain of self-help literature. The risk of sailing that close is unavoidable. Plato, Aristotle, Emerson, Kant, Schopenhauer, Nietzsche have a touch of the self-help in their deepest philosophies. It is what makes them useful to us. It is the accessible element that encourages us to explore deeper the more abstruse areas of their philosophy. This is said only to suggest that there is much in these dialogues that one can take away on an individual, intimate level; much that is helpful, amid the intellectual reaches and the more academic references.

The macro world of the culture, of activism, of Rowan William's support for Extinction Rebellion, of anxieties about the divisiveness of Brexit, of the failure to listen in contemporary politics, the lack of world class leadership, conflict resolution, the necessities for the education of the emotion and the imagination, the grim realities of war and social crisis are woven into a humane tapestry of concerns.

As you read you wonder if they will solve the world's problems, if they will they come up with workable answers. This gives a kind of propulsion to the book and is a reminder that good conversation by its very nature is dynamic. These conversations are so thoughtful, their spark and connections so delightful that you don't want them to end, for they are rich in facts and ideas.

Rowan Williams is always careful to avoid the sentimentality of ideas that are popular but contain some truth, and one can sense his refusal also to be cowed by the truth of an emotion. Always he comes back, like a poet, to things. Ideas are tactile for him. He comes back to the reality of things and to the truth of his faith. But he wears his faith lightly, not defensively, but rather as a final place of rest, a comfort offered, but not asserted. His respect for other religious traditions is profoundly evident.

One might ask if in these dialogues they give us practical actions to tackle the challenges talked about? But that would be the wrong question. They do not give answers as such. They provide an orientation. They offer better questions. They present a more intelligent framing of the questions. They gift us new perspectives.

The trouble with answers is that they are often facile. They are often not deep enough. More commonly they prove to be the wrong answers. If you have not asked the right question, any answer would be the wrong answer. The right question almost begins to answer itself.

Answers are terminal. Questions are probing, tentative, exploratory, investigative. Questions keep going to the roots, to the causes, to the heart of situations.

Dialogue best responds to the fluidity of the human condition. The word dialogue is itself a dialogue between two words, dia and logos.

Tremendous complexity emerges when you bring these two words together. Dia in Greek means through, between, across. But the real richness comes when we consider the Greek word logos which means variously discourse, word, account, reason, proportion, to mention a few. For Heraclitus it was a higher principle of knowledge and harmony. In the Gospel according to John it referred to the divine word, the Word incarnate.

These dialogues hint at all of these things, the human dimension of reason, the divine dimension of grace, the practical value of being open and the spiritual value of finding a new harmony in our troubled world.

That Rowan Williams, a man of intellect and faith and Mary Zournazi, an atheist and humanist, could come together in a spirit of inquiry is in itself a sign of hope for our times.

ACKNOWLEDGEMENTS

We are grateful to the colleagues, friends and students who have inspired us over the years during the formation and writing of this book. With many thanks to Liza Thompson who was originally receptive to our proposal for such a collaborative book, and who took the risk to publish it. Thanks very much to Lucy Russell and Lisa Goodrum who have helped us to see this book through to publication. We are especially grateful to Camille Nurka for her assistance and copy editing in the final stages of writing this manuscript.

Rowan is indebted to conversations over several years with colleagues and friends including Nicholas Boyle, James Mumford, Richard Sennett, Charles Taylor, and among his research students, Gus Howard and Ragnar Bergem. Mary would like to also thank Christos Tsiolkas for sharing some wonderful conversations over the years on ethics, love and the works of Saint Paul.

Prologue

Some Reflections on Justice and Love

On trial

One of the starting points for this book came out of a personal experience that made me consider questions of justice and where justice can sometimes fail. In the last years of his life, my father lived with dementia. His world became consumed, more and more, by extraordinary moments of joy and anger, sadness and fear, and his imagination flourished as his body became less able to navigate the world and its meanings. He would chant Homeric-style verse in a loud and unabashedly oratorical voice in the middle of a living room, at the dinner table or lying in his bed. His stories had no coherence except in his own poetic verse, which was ever-present and meaningful to him.

In the midst of this experience, my father was caught in a long and drawn-out battle over conflicting ideas of moral value and worth in the light of changing filial relations. There was a struggle over who had the 'right' to take care of him and the legacies of inheritance, both literal and figurative, that brought into sharp focus the often unwelcome, selfish and complex side of human relations. The struggle for justice seemed to be reduced to the legacies of power and old familial relations.

During a tribunal hearing that took place over the rights to his care, different family members came forward to declare their loyalties and stakeholder interests. As the tribunal progressed, my father became increasingly agitated as the words spoken *to* and *about* him turned into threatening sounds and meaningless babble. He began to silently weep. There are no scales of justice that can be called to measure the 'right' or the wrong in this situation – where the patriarch, unbeknownst to himself, is on trial, and when the trauma and fantasy of entitlement are played out in selfish ways and the reality of the person, and their experience, is diminished.

In some ways, the story is a strangely perverse inversion of Shakespeare's *King Lear*.[1] In Shakespeare's tale, an ageing patriarch, in exchange for declarations of love and affinity, divides his estate among his three daughters. In this tragedy, the love that is proclaimed toward King Lear by the two sisters Regan and Goneril has nothing to do with the love which respects the duty and obligations to a father; the youngest daughter, Cordelia, is banished forever by Lear for her lack of fidelity understood in such terms. As the two older sisters plot against Lear and each other in their desire for power, Lear is left without any authority or dignity. He eventually goes mad. Both the fictional King Lear and the real-life story demonstrate how we can often lose sight of the 'suffering' of the other when the world is conceived in this fashion – where the debt of love is tied up with the debts of power and economic exchange, and where the tenets of law and the formation of justice seem inseparable. In reality, we know what might be 'just' and 'moral' do not always come together, in the legal sense of the word.

In the tragedy of *King Lear*, we can recognise the stories of our own lives and the political machinations that shape the world when the sense of entitlement and right takes over, and 'market' value and power is infused with betrayal and deceit; and how those most at risk are people who no longer have 'power' in the marketplace and political debate. In the real-life drama, the father as a confused patriarch became part of an exchange value that exposed the limits of law as it collided with (in)justice, in both personal and public ways.

The philosopher, mystic and political activist Simone Weil provides a useful distinction between the sense of individual entitlement and right, and the experience of suffering. She states:

Justice consists in seeing that no harm is done to men. Whenever a man cries inwardly: 'Why am I being hurt?' harm is being done to him. He is often mistaken when he tries to define the harm, and why and by whom it is being inflicted on him. But the cry itself is infallible.

The other cry, which we hear so often: 'Why has somebody else got more than I have?', refers to rights. We must learn to distinguish between the two cries and to do all that is possible, as gently as possible, to hush the second one, with the help of the code of justice, regular tribunals and the police. Minds capable of solving problems of this kind can be formed in a law school.

But the cry 'Why am I being hurt?' raises quite different problems, for which the spirit of truth, justice and love is indispensable.[2]

As Weil reminds us, rights understood without a spirit of attention and love 'evoke a latent war and awaken the spirit of contention. To place the notion of rights at the centre of social conflicts is to inhibit any possible impulse of charity on both sides'.[3] Justice, then, needs the impulse of charity and other such virtues.

But how do we ethically respond to and address people's injustices, their suffering and their privation? Historically speaking, Mahatma Gandhi, Martin Luther King and other activists have inspired these concerns of charity, truth and justice through different types of non-violent action and the acknowledgement of the spiritual dimension as a kind of public and political necessity. This is not so much a dogma of truth, but an ethical approach that recognises the value of human and non-human life and the relations that can arise out of communion and solidarity.

These questions have grown more urgent in the late capitalist era, in which a market society, as Michael Sandel has put it, does not equate with a just society.[4] At the forefront of this book, then, is how to open out the question of justice to incorporate different virtues and values. The quest for the spiritual dimension to our lives need not necessarily be religious, but we may learn a lot from different theological and philosophical languages, which together create imaginative approaches that can help us to navigate and strengthen the social bonds that connect us, rather than tear us apart.

After life

I would suggest that Ricky Gervais's *After Life* television series offers similar concerns: that is, how to understand different moral and social virtues, especially when confronted by death and when self-absorption and narcissism is at the forefront of one's world.[5] After the death of his wife, journalist Tony Johnson (played by Gervais) contemplates suicide and the meaninglessness of life. His wife appears to him in the 'after life' – the after life, in this instance, is her video recordings and counsel to him about how to live and how to be involved in life despite his usual selfish behaviour. Her counsel seems to offer him the opportunity to think about the 'good', and the joy in life, and how to reorient his life amid his grief. One of the main reasons for Tony to keep living is the responsibility he has toward his dog and the stories that he collects for his local newspaper, which document the lives of other people and their unique traits, and the often strange and wonderful ways in which they make sense of the world.

Gervais's fundamental concern is with the need for an ethical life in the here and now, and it is an important provocation in reconfiguring moral value and worth in our complex personal and social lives. Like Gervais, I am not religious, but having been raised Greek Orthodox, and after the death of my father, I found myself taken by rituals that surround death. I found moments of solace within them. I became fascinated by, and drawn to, holy places, not necessarily for the sermons, but for the space in which to stop and breathe, to be with the grief that was overtaking me and the tragedy I had witnessed during the time of my father's illness and the decline in filial relationships.

The moments of ritual enabled me to contemplate how we might consider our everyday responses to the world, and how, especially, to re-imagine some of these important rituals and ideas that religions have given to us that may offer solace in times of sorrow and in times of need.

Although Gervais's character may not state it this way, the show offers forms of 'recognition' that lean toward, and may also be part of, a religious vocabulary. It is about the experience of grief and the need to understand the different values of kindness, compassion and care that can occur in our own lives. Even the most ardent secularists, such as Gervais, would consider how such approaches to life did not just fall out of the sky, but have emerged out of the histories and development of various philosophical and religious traditions. As Charles Taylor reminds us, the secular, as we live it, has materialised through a variety of social, historical and cultural practices – in other words, many diverse systems of belief have emerged through different time periods and social organisations.[6]

In this regard, the pronouncement that 'god is perhaps dead' from philosophies as diverse as Hegel and Nietzsche point us toward the need to cultivate new habits of thought and morality, and this is something that is emergent with, and part of, the historical changes in systems of belief. It could be argued that the cultivation of new habits involves the recognition of modes of thinking and approaches to ethical life that come before and after the rise of modernity, and the formation of our contemporary lives.

Philosophers from Aristotle to contemporary thinkers such as Alasdair McIntyre have considered how justice is part of a virtuous life and how the narratives we tell about ourselves and our sense of belonging can become foundational to the ways we might perceive and understand a language of justice.[7] As Michael Sandel has reflected, the theories of justice, from Kant to Rawls, insist upon the universality and dignity of humans and the freedom to choose; but, at the same time, their ideas of right as prior to the 'good' may not always guide us toward the best ways to live.[8] There is a need to consider how we understand those moments of despair and tragedy that are part of the stories and experiences that are individually lived but collectively shared.

Iris Murdoch's work is useful in this context. Her book *The Sovereignty of Good* is an attempt to explore matters of justice that integrate the imagination and the idea of the *good*, to show how moving toward the good can reorient cultural habits, allowing us to perceive justly.[9] Her philosophy opens up some questions and negotiations of what an ethical and virtuous life might involve – how we might be able to make ourselves better people, and how storytelling and imagination might help us to understand the fabric of our individual and social lives, both in its mystery and value. As Murdoch writes:

> We use our imagination not to escape the world but to join it, and this exhilarates us because of the distance between the ordinary dulled consciousness and an apprehension of the real. The value concepts are here patently tied on to the world, they are stretched as it were between the truth-seeking mind and the world, they are not moving about on their own as adjuncts of the personal will. The authority of morals is the authority of truth, that is of reality. We can see the length, the extension, of these concepts as patient attention

transforms accuracy without interval into just discernment. Here too we can see it as natural to the particular kind of creatures that we are that love should be inseparable from justice, and clear vision from respect for the real.[10]

Ideas of justice may hinge, then, on the necessity of enjoining reality with imagination to provide the care and attention that we need to challenge the injustices that surround us. This book orients itself toward questions of how we might enjoin reality with imagination to consider possibilities for thinking and feeling differently about our social realities and to offer alternative visions of the world.

Reckoning

Frantz Fanon's *The Wretched of the Earth* is concerned with the dispossessed and questions of justice, both in the context of our entwined colonial histories and in how we address the 'wretchedness' within our individual lives.[11] How do we recognise the multiple roles we may inhabit as oppressor and/or oppressed, and the legacies of histories that we have inherited? There is a scene that always sticks in my mind from the film *Battle of Algiers*: a bomb goes off in the middle of the French quarter.[12] Several blocks away, a local worker is on the street attending to his work and minding his own business. In the aftermath of the bomb, chaos erupts. The police and the people in the French quarter are yelling and screaming; the police are frantically looking for the culprits. The worker is caught in the groundswell of anger and chaos, and as he starts to feel the anger of the crowd, he panics and tries to flee the violence and hatred. The confusion is marked on his face. He is arrested and subsequently charged for the explosion: he was in the wrong place at the wrong time. This is the kind of violence where the everyday person is caught in a logic of power and force that often has very little to do with their own direct experience and lived reality. These are the crimes of history and the perpetual circuits of violence.

In her essay 'The Iliad or the Poem of Force', Weil argues that nobody wins in a game of force and violence.[13] What violence does is to limit a person's ability to 'consent', or their 'power to refuse', as Weil states it. In other words, the power to refuse acknowledges the need to stop the perpetuation of violence, but at the same time, it necessitates that people have access to safe conditions and opportunities so that the refusal is a real option. Any form of institutional or structural violence that does not allow the power to refuse renders people speechless; as is most often the case, people who are caught in the crossfire cannot 'refuse' the violence done them, and this is the extreme form of injustice. There is a need to encourage a language of justice which holds, as Weil has suggested, that no 'harm' be done to any man or woman, and this would also mean any sentient or non-sentient life. A just society curtails the force of violence through allowing the power to refuse it. This involves both individual as well as societal potential, so that no force is held over a country or a people, and that a person's destitution is not ignored.

Today, we cannot think about this power to refuse that citizenship should confirm without coming up against the figure of the stranger – the migrant, the refugee. In the political sphere, as the philosopher Hannah Arendt has argued, the 'rights of man', as it played out in the twentieth century (and now the twenty-first century), has led to the increased violation of stateless people and refugees.[14] If the stateless person no longer has the right to be a citizen, and by the same logic they do not share the rights of man, they are not given the *right* to be human. Fanon, Weil and Arendt, in their different ways, are addressing the violence of derealisation on the part of sovereign states and laws that refuse to recognise the human value of peoples classed as non-citizens. The human 'cry' that makes us all too human – the love and loss that we all share and experience – is denied, and the refusal of rights, in this sense, forecloses the potential for human dignity. The philosopher Judith Butler has put to us: 'What makes for a grievable life?'[15] It is this very question that must make us confront the destitution of others.[16] It is a reality that the global stranger is no longer on the other side of the world, but is part of the dispossession and displacement which has made up the human histories of this planet.

The issue of how to address the destitution and derealisation of others is central to the conversations on justice and love throughout this book, and the framework for understanding what's at stake today when we consider what community and identity might mean in local and global contexts.

Grace

In the *King Lear* tragedy, there is a moment of grace that transpires between Lear and Cordelia at a crucial juncture in the play. Both are imprisoned because of the fear and treachery of the sisters and their husbands in their desire for power. Cordelia forgives Lear for his banishment of her, and they spend moments of real joy together, but her fate is sealed by her untimely death and execution. Perhaps we are all on trial for crimes we did not commit, and in some ways, the legacies of history – the personal and political affronts – bear witness to the sorrows of each of us, while at the same time, to the wretchedness in our own hearts in local and global ways. Cordelia is perhaps the epitome of the healer in that sense, a figure who shows the loving side of grace and mercy despite all odds.

As tragedy often shows, grace happens in ways that remind us that the world *may not be as it seems*, and it is through this recognition that we may become aware of other realities and ways of living. The American novelist Flannery O'Connor brings some of the awe of grace into light as both a religious writer and novelist. She has written that the 'beginning of human knowledges is through the senses and the fiction writer begins where human perception begins'.[17] In more general terms, O'Connor notes that the 'habits of art', following from the philosopher Jacques Maritain, are to do just this: to bring us to truth. Art, in this sense, can shock us or bring to our attention elements of injustices that we might choose otherwise to ignore or dismiss.

Authors such as Fyodor Dostoevsky and many others help us to navigate the 'trials' and tragedies that make up our everyday lives, and may 'shock' us out of our complicity. Most recently, we see this approach in the Australian author Christos Tsiolkas's book *Damascus* on the reckoning of Saint Paul, and the different moments of grace that led Paul toward an ethical life, and the basis of a universal Christian ethic.[18] Such novels shock us in different ways, as all good works of art do, as they provide us with a lens into reality. It is in the realm of art that tragedy and imagination can reach into a human experience that may otherwise be outcast from discourses of language and power.

These habits of art relate to questions of beauty and to the just. As the author Elaine Scarry proposes, the etymological history of beauty links to the very formation of the concept of justice. She suggests that beauty is linked to the appeal to 'fairness', which acknowledges our sensory perceptions; with its 'direct appeal to the senses, beauty stops us, transfixes us, fills us with a "surfeit of aliveness".[19] Similarly, Simone Weil has written that this attention to life is about living in the 'bare instant' of it, the 'pure and instantaneous present' which opens out the space of time and encounter. This involves a perceptual awareness that brings together the everyday and the mysterious qualities of beauty, enabling a different response to the world that derives from curiosity and attention, rather than self-interest and indifference. As the poet Rainer Maria Rilke has written, beauty is both awesome and terrifying; in this sense, 'fairness' and beauty relate to justice not as a balance of scales, but as an alignment to what we encounter in this world that may not be pretty, or fair.[20]

This attention to the world provides moments of grace, mercy and justice that bestow us with a different way to respond and act in the world. These are the lessons of Lear and the wretchedness in our own hearts and minds that require us to recognise the limits of own constructions of 'good and evil', in which doing justice is not about vengeance or punishment, but about seeing relationships as they are and working from there. As Murdoch has written, the love which brings a right answer is an exercise of justice and realism, and really *looking*.[21] It is this consideration of love and 'justly looking' that concerns us here.

Love

The love to which Murdoch refers as an exercise of justice involves not treating people as objects but as people, and this recovers a sense of dignity that can be lost when justice is devoid of this realm of attention in both personal and political ways. In *Antigone*, the well-known play by Sophocles, we see some of the tensions between the divine realm and individual and social fate.[22] Antigone wishes to bury her dead brother who is seen as a traitor to the state. Both her brothers die fighting each other; one is named a hero, the other is considered a traitor by Creon, the new King of Thebes. To bury a traitor is against the rules and regulations of the law of the state, and the 'law' is embodied by the character of King Creon. Regardless, Antigone is fulfilling her obligation and filial respect, love and duty, to her brother. Creon thinks she is mad for not upholding the regulation of the state, as she is, in effect, moving outside of law. For Hegel, the play exposes the confused and narrow approaches that the characters inhabit, which lead them both to destruction and tragedy.

As the philosopher Martha Nussbaum has argued, in tragedy and in everyday life we need imagination in order for us to inhabit and recognise the fate of others.[23] What Antigone personifies is a love that has no boundaries and that moves beyond the limits of law, or rather, the appeal to something larger than ourselves that empowers us to recognise the human dignity of others. The works of love, as Raimond

Gaita has called them, involve the opportunities to respond justly with dignity to the 'affliction of others',[24] and this is what moves us to come closer to different ethical choices. This echoes Simone Weil's account that in the ancient Greek mind, there was no language of 'rights', but rather, a language of justice that can evolve out of the recognition of love. Antigone declares: 'I was born to share, not hate, but love.'[25]

I often think of Antigone as an anti-war heroine par excellence – a heroine who operates in the realm of love that moves across and beyond the limits of law and forces us, in some ways, to challenge our own limits in the recognition of the dignity and lives of others. This evokes the works of Saint Paul and his ethics, and the idea of 'right' in the Greek sense of *dikaios*, which is about both a sense of the just and a gesture toward a form of truthfulness and reckoning, which does not absolve us of guilt, but realises that love – in both individual and social senses – requires an understanding that moves beyond our limited sense of identity.[26]

*

Returning to one of the starting points for this book and the domain of justice and love, I turn to Bertolt Brecht's play *The Caucasian Chalk Circle* (the ending is loosely drawn on the biblical tale of the Judgement of Solomon), which provides some insight into the necessity of love over self-interest and parodies some of the machinations of law.[27] The play is a parable about a peasant woman who rescues a baby from a wealthy and corrupt landowner and legislator. The two female protagonists are Natella, the Governor's wife, and Grusha, her maid. In the midst of a revolution that sees the beheading of her husband, the Governor, Natella abandons her child and Grusha takes the child into her care. After the revolution and the restoration of the old regime, Natella returns to claim her son so as to maintain power and the inheritance of the family estate; her son is the sole heir of the estate and family fortune, and she cannot access it without him.

Grusha and Natella stand trial against each other on the 'ownership' of the child. The presiding judge, Azdek, who is known for taking bribes and drinking on the job, draws a circle and places the child in its centre. He states that the true mother will pull the child from the circle, but if they both pull at once, they will tear the child in half (perhaps more brutally in the biblical story, Solomon suggests cutting the child in half and that each woman would receive half the child). As with the judgement of Solomon, the woman who can truly 'see' what's at stake refuses to act in such a way that will bring harm to the child; and Grusha, in this case, is prepared to give up the child because of her love for him. She is given the final judgement to keep the child as the 'true mother', and the judge declares that the child's inheritance will be dissolved and it will be given over to the city. In this instance, Grusha exercises a love that transcends her personal want and provides the condition for a form of justice that does not enforce retribution or violence, but is, rather, the love which brings the exercise of 'justice and realism'.

As a philosopher and filmmaker, much of my interest in these themes and questions of justice and love arises from a lifelong commitment to, and investigation of, hope, war and peace, and how creativity and art can allow us to bear 'witness' to the realities that confront us. I invited the theologian, poet and author Rowan Williams to join me on this quest to explore the relationship between justice and love, and to pursue the theological and philosophical underpinnings that may help us to enrich a language of justice. Rowan's writings and work on theological, literary and poetical forms of understanding ourselves and the world provide a fruitful ground for this collaboration. Together, informed by our different backgrounds, we try to respond to the complexities of human life and how to approach the making of a just world.

Throughout the conversations, we are inspired by a variety of writers, theologians, philosophers, artists and poets in opening out a series of questions and reflections about how we might consider justice and individual and social action. This book is not about criminal justice, or distributive justice, or procedural justice, in the usual sense of the term; instead, it offers other accounts of 'justice' that grapple with human suffering and the tragedy that surrounds our everyday lives. While the book acknowledges different forms of injustice, abuse and corruption across a range of social institutions, including the church, the focus here is primarily on ways to respond to the circuits of violence and denial that are part of any form of abuse.

This book is divided into three parts and covers a period of five years, where we met to discuss our concerns around justice. At the same time, we became 'witnesses' to events as they unfolded, such as the Syrian refugee crisis, Paris bombings, ISIS attacks, Brexit, US elections, the ongoing concern for the environment, and the impact of social and economic crisis worldwide. Our conversations are about modes of engagement to facilitate ways of thinking about these issues, and I would suggest that in general, this is what conversations can do for us: they can allow us to *think about thinking* and *to think together* to broaden our world views. By 'thinking together', Rowan and I have tried to create some new meanings, questions and approaches to justice, and we invite readers to *think along with us* and to raise some of their own questions and approaches to justice and love.

The task of this book, then, is to work toward learning and unlearning habits of mind and culture; to think through questions of time, grace, mercy and forgiveness, and how the present may offer the means for living in the now rather than a future-oriented world; and to create a space in which those claims to the sacred are not solely in the realm of the religious person but are part of our secular lives, whether we like it or not. This is about activating the richness of our imaginations and acknowledging the qualities that we share that may allow us to think toward our local *and* global futures together. This feels alarmingly real to me in the unprecedented heat, bushfires and toxic smoke that are surrounding me in Sydney at present, and the urgent need to think together, not only for ourselves, but for the planet. As Frantz Fanon reminds us, each generation must fulfil its mission or betray it. I hope the conversations in this book are a small step toward fulfilling the task that lies ahead of us.

Mary Zournazi
Sydney, Australia, and Athens, Greece
December/January 2020

PART ONE

JUSTLY LOOKING

In this part, Rowan and I explore together some philosophical and theological thinking around justice to set the context for the book. We disentangle ideas of justice from senses of individual entitlement and right, and we investigate the idea of justice as a virtue and how this approach to justice has to do with *seeing fairly* or *seeing wholly*, which is a *qualitative* way of perceiving and understanding what is just. This is an invitation to the imagination and how to rethink 'doing justice' through different values and virtues. We explore some of the ideas of Saint Paul and other theological thinkers in considering how to approach what is 'just' and 'diabolical' in our lives.

We call upon on various literary, artistic and cultural practices that enable us to *justly look* at the world to reflect upon what this might mean for ideas of the 'good' in our lives today. Through some of Shakespeare's plays and different literary texts, we address the limits of mercy, law and justice, and through artists such as Cézanne and Monet, we think about the perceptual quality of seeing and justice.

As novelist and painter John Berger once wrote, to paint the existent may be one of the last revolutionary acts. It promises the potential of hope, and it is in this manner that we consider that to see the world *wholly* or *fairly* requires this attention to detail and fact. This may be some of the real evidence that we need to address and respond to the suffering as well as the joy in our lives and the lives of others.

I

On Justice

April 2015

MZ   Let's start these conversations with the etymology of 'justice' – it has Latin roots, right?

RW   It's Latin, yes, and related to the idea of *jus* – meaning law, or 'right'. This is slightly different from the way in which it works in Greek and Hebrew. The Hebrew, *tzedakah*, has more the sense of 'alignment', a 'rightness' of posture, or direction, perhaps. And a bit of that comes over in the Greek *dikaios* as well. If the Latin *justitia* and *justus* bring to mind the sense of resorting to or relating to the law, you don't quite get that in Greek or Hebrew. It's a more intrinsic thing, I think. To act with justice, in Hebrew, or to *do* justice, is to align yourself properly; it is not so much to do with settling a claim.

MZ   I think that's really important, that reminder of an alignment to something as opposed to a settling of a dispute. When do you think that moment happened, where the settling of a dispute came into the language as 'justice'?

RW   I don't know. But I think any language that depends on Latin, any culture that depends on Roman culture, is going to be inheriting something of that distributive or apportioning sense, the conflict-settling side of it; it is why, historically, when the Greek New Testament gets into Latin, all sorts of ideas about what's involved in the 'righteousness' of God change their emphasis and you get a much stronger emphasis, in Latin theology, on satisfying claims and settling things.

MZ   If you were to go and think more about the Greek and the Hebrew, then you'd have this sense of 'alignment', or what is 'right'.

RW   Yes. If you think of how Saint Paul speaks about the righteousness of God, and how we are made righteous, it's not so much how we are made compliant with law, but how we're made compatible – if that's the word – with God.

MZ   If it's not about being lawful or law-abiding, then we are looking at something more robust and interesting that aligns us with a different sense of what justice might involve.

RW   I suppose you could say that the problem, as Saint Paul himself sees it, is this: he has recognised that simply keeping to the law doesn't in itself deliver 'righteousness', in the sense of becoming aligned or compatible with God. So you can clock up all the particular acts that you've done rightly, but you won't actually achieve real 'justice' – because that is your compatibility with the life of God, your capacity to live in God's company without agony or shame. God's rightness, or right-directedness, makes demands on your right-directedness, but you can't put them together just by law-keeping. The whole problem about the Christian understanding of justice has roots somewhere in that complex of thought.

MZ Yes. There seems to have been a historic split, between 'rightness' and law, when the law became an entity in itself from the sixteenth century onwards.

RW Increasingly so, yes. Especially once 'rights' are understood as certain specific entitlements.

MZ Yes. So that's what I'm really wanting to get at: what is that difference in approaching rights? That is, between the former sense of the right direction – which seems, to me, to be the one that offers the possibility of 'communion' or a relationship – and the individual sense of *my* rights, or entitlement to things. In the latter way of thinking, the *person* becomes the centre of everything.

RW That's right. I was thinking about the different ways in which we use 'doing justice' to something or someone. We might say, 'That photograph doesn't do justice to him'. What does that mean? Not that some claim has been left unfulfilled, but that the photograph doesn't allow the person to be seen as they should be. And that's much more on the relational end of the spectrum, rather than the problem-solving or conflict-settling end. It's not that a photographer or a portrait painter has somehow failed to pay his or her dues. They've just not *seen* something, they've not been on the proper wavelength.

MZ Yes. And similarly, I think, if you're looking at a portrait or a painting or an image, you're wanting to see something and attribute something, whereas there might be something you *see* that isn't in the framework that you're bringing with you, something you're not expecting from the image. So it's not necessarily the unspoken, it's something to do with the spirit in which you enter or relate to the image.

RW   Essentially, it's to do with how you want to *see* what's before you. There are ways of trying to see that seek to contain or swallow things, and there are ways of seeing that allow the vision to be sent off in different directions and filling out what's there.

MZ   Yes. And the imagination comes into play.

RW   And the imagination, yes. It's one reason why portrait-painting fascinates me. My sister-in-law's a painter and most of her work is portraiture – almost entirely of people she knows very well. I often look at her work and think of it in terms of this 'doing justice'. In some respects, she's not what you'd call a realistic portrait painter, but what she produces are quite obviously *portraits*; they are very definitely ways of seeing what's there, and they often have an indeterminacy in them that allows you to see more as you look again. That's why – for her, as for other painters and portraitists – often a sketch will do better 'justice' than a full-scale oil painting. It can be very illuminating to think about what it means to say, in that context, that an image 'does justice'.

MZ   Yes, doing justice. This is something interesting that Roland Barthes talked about in his book *Camera Lucida*, and his search for the 'just' image of his mother.[1] He was looking at photographs after she died, looking for images of her, and he found one photo from when she was a child (what he called the Wintergarden photograph), and it was a surprise to him. What he found in it was a sort of kindness in her hands, things like this; he found a tenderness in her through the photograph and he didn't expect to see her like that. He wanted a 'just' image of his mother and he found it in unexpectedly in that photograph. And this surprise or unexpectedness has something to do with the ability to see. So maybe there is something in that. But to do justice is wanting a result, isn't it, in some ways? You're wanting some kind of definitive result, some finality – something which, actually, is never the case.

RW Yes. The trouble with starting from the legal claim end of the spectrum is that in those terms it *is* possible to 'finish the business' – or, at least, it seems to be, though it isn't so in practice, of course. In fact, this is the kind of illusion that's quite cruel to people who feel that the law is going to deliver closure for them. 'The killer of my daughter has gone to prison and now that's all settled'; but it isn't. To claim that it is, is certainly one approach to the doing of justice but not a particularly interesting one, in some ways, and certainly not a very decisive one. It does a bit of necessary business, but it can't be the whole picture.

MZ I think the clue is in what you were just saying. The law has its function, but the truth is that it's never going to satisfy, in some respects, because it's not going to deal with the emotional trauma of what's happened, or other things that may arise … and there's the question of what happens when justice fails? I think ideas of justice and law are necessary, but that there is something else that needs to be addressed in the understanding of *what is just* or *what is justice*?

RW   And because that's potentially a really enormous issue, it is alarming for people. It seems a lot easier just to tick off the things that have been 'settled'.

MZ   Yet it's that approach that creates the problems.

RW   This is a particularly interesting question for me at the moment in the context of the development charity I chair. In Christian Aid, we've been having quite a lot of discussion over the last few years about the need to move from the language of charity to the language of justice, because we don't want to see international aid as 'charity', in the sense of a nice thing to do with our surplus, kindly throwing coins to the poor, as it were. It's about what is properly *due* to the deprived and disadvantaged; and I think all of us have wanted to say, as many Christians would want to say, 'Yes, of course.' But what we're in the business of is rather more than simply rectifying a balance, or clearing the slate, or paying our debts. The justice we want to affirm and sustain can't simply turn its back on the proper root of charity – the element that has to do with mending relations and so on.

MZ   What is coming to mind is if we go back to the proper root of charity, it opens up something interesting, and, in a way, that has to be thought through in relationship to justice.

RW   Exactly.

MZ   And how would we begin that understanding without dismissing either? I can see the discussions that could go on in an organisational context: there would be a limit to how you could intervene and what you can do; but if you're thinking about the *core* of the idea of charity and the *core* of the idea of justice, which are very different things to the way we popularly consider them ...

RW   Yes. Both words have come down in the world and got into bad company.

MZ   Charity in particular.

RW   I read something on this years ago in some of John Bossy's work on seventeenth-century society: one of the points he makes is that 'charity' in the Middle Ages is one of the words you would use for whatever it is in a society that controls rivalry, that resettles proper mutual bonds.[2]

MZ   That's very interesting and very different from the usual sense of the word today.

RW   And, in fact, it has an element of *justice* in it, in the wider sense we've been discussing. One of the things that happens with church festivals in the Middle Ages is that people have a chance to put their relationships straight, to realign their relationships, and that's regarded as an act of *charity* – not charity as giving to the poor, but charity as settling more deeply into where you are. It's this use of the word that you find in the Book of Common Prayer, in the invitation to all who 'are in love and charity with their neighbours'. I don't think that just means you *feel* benevolently about the people next door. As the Exhortation to those who are going to receive Communion says in the prayer book, it's about managing your relationships in such a way that they're not asymmetrical or oppressive. There's a reference in the earliest version of this text to doing something about 'other men's lands or goods unlawfully withholden'. Charity is what rectifies that kind of relation.

MZ   So it's not conflict resolution as we usually understand it, but it has a function that relates a bit to that.

RW   Certainly. It's a way of limiting a spiral of inequity.

MZ   So when you say this about the religious festivals, how exactly would they negotiate this charity? The image is coming into focus, but I'm not sure I quite get a sense of what was happening. I haven't thought about it in that way and I imagine most people haven't.

RW   John Bossy is worth looking at on this. Without going into all the detail, what he points out is that in the fifteenth century in the cities, for a feast like Corpus Christi, the great mid-summer celebration, the trade guilds would get together to put on a big event for the city. It would often involve performing the great mystery plays and the story of salvation; but it would also include sacramental drama in church and distribution to the poor. It was all a large-scale shared event of making peace and restoring or affirming balance, or equity, for the wider community.

MZ   So how are people involved? How are the poor also involved in this?

RW   You might say that 'the poor' are still *objects* in this scheme rather than agents; it's still close to some of the problems in our modern picture there. But at least the emphasis is not so much on just giving to the poor, it's on somehow putting things straight.

MZ From the point of view of those who don't have the access or the resources or whatever, what does charity mean for them in that context? Because I think if it is about a 'settling' in some sense, perhaps not quite the one we're used to, there must be some other way of understanding this experience . . .

RW I suppose, ideally, it would mean that the poor would see that they have a guaranteed place in the order of things, that they're not 'superfluous people'. This doesn't take you anything like far enough, granted, but there is some 'covenantal' obligation recognised. The poor are not just left out of the picture as an embarrassing extra.

MZ I'm thinking about the virtues here, thinking about the traditional 'theological' virtues of faith, hope and charity – they've all got their problems in one way or another. If charity is a virtue, then it does involve ethical action, right? Which also involves a person-to-person, a human-to-human way of relating, as well as something beyond . . .

RW Very much so.

MZ So people in this medieval context are acting in charity. It's a way of responding.

RW As a virtue, charity is a disposition to act in a certain way – and that's why justice also is a virtue. It is one of the four 'cardinal' virtues: temperance, prudence, fortitude and justice. So, moderation in your attitudes and desires – temperance; the proper adjustment of means to ends – prudence; courage and persistence in pursuing the right – fortitude; and the capacity to give each their due – justice. These are habits of temperament, fixed attitudes, dispositions. They plug the discussion into a wider system of understanding human nature, so that these 'cardinal' virtues, the virtues that are the 'hinge', *cardo*, of good action, open out onto the theological virtues. You can't just isolate justice from that context of human maturation.

MZ   What I'm interested in is how we open out these virtues in a public sense. How do we work with them, wherever we come from, whether we're religious or not? I feel these are virtues that have gone out of focus for us, but it is important to consider how they work, just as with charity.

RW   I think 'virtue' is a key word here. I suppose it's why people in the last few decades have been getting more and more interested in 'virtue ethics', rather than ethics as just about isolated decision making. The question becomes, 'What sort of actions and dispositions make you this or that sort of person?', rather than, 'How do you solve this or that problem? What's the right answer to this and the right answer to that?' If you want some kind of continuity in your self-understanding, you need to understand what virtue is; and if you start from the idea of justice as a virtue, and perhaps maybe a virtue which is to do with *seeing fairly* or *seeing wholly*, this may be transformative here.

MZ   There is something important in *seeing fairly* or *seeing wholly* and it is a very different form of perceiving and responding to reality.

RW   And it's a *qualitative* perceiving in some way. That's where I'd go back to what we were saying about portraits.

MZ Can we talk a bit more about 'seeing fairly'? I'm thinking about Elaine Scarry's work and how she links the aesthetic (that is, beauty) to the obligation to justice. She argues that 'fairness' has an etymological link to the aesthetic sense: what's 'fair' is what attracts our attention, our aliveness to the world, and it is in this way that justice and beauty line up together. Is this something qualitatively different from or larger than just 'alignment'?

RW It's very much a dimension of what we might mean by 'alignment' in the widest sense. We're talking about the harmonics of action, to use another kind of metaphor – that which doesn't jar us or give us a feeling of violent disruption going on. And I think that's completely in line with this stress on the aesthetic.

*

MZ Let's take this forward in the context of law breaking down: what are the resources that enable us to see afresh what justice could mean in such an environment?

RW Law can break down in many ways; and when law has been reduced simply to the settling of claims, there is a sort of breakdown there. One thing that strikes me about our very litigious contemporary society, here in the United Kingdom and in the United States, say, and in much of the 'developed' world, is an increasing tendency to think everything must be settleable in terms of disputed claims. There are no accidents and there are no forgivables. There is always clearly identifiable fault or tort or debt; and that has to be the default setting for understanding every situation. But this suggests precisely a lack of resources for thinking about justice – a real emptying out of what the word could positively mean and a loss of understanding of the virtues in the way we've been talking about them. It's a worrying place to be.

MZ   It's true, because it limits how people can interact with each other. I am thinking of very ordinary experiences – my father, when he was in residential care, the residents couldn't make cups of tea because of the threat of litigious action if they spilled hot water on themselves. Of course, that could be an issue, but it seems that you can't act in more ordinary ways because you're worried about a legal threat against you.

RW   Yes, and you're encouraged to be thinking, Am I getting my rights? Am I getting my dues? In some circumstances, that's an absolutely necessary question, where there's manifest justice and violence; but it's the leakage of that into every single relationship that suggests something's gone really quite badly askew in how we think about *what is just*. It's the reduction of everything almost to the adolescent cry, 'Everything is so unfair!'

MZ   What about the other virtues we've mentioned? How does justice fit with them?

RW   A *just* temperament would mean you had a well-developed instinct for the appropriate, the apt way of treating people. And that temperament would depend on your having the other virtues as well. You would need to know how to work out how you treat people, to have a sort of feel for how people should be treated, and for this, you then need *prudence*, because you need to think, 'All right, how do I actually bring my intentions to effect in a sensible way?' So I look at someone and think, 'justly', that they need love and attention. Do I then go and empty my bank balance and pour it into their lap? Will that be the most effective response? Will it change what needs changing?

MZ So there's discernment needed.

RW Yes, you need discernment, and that is the exercise of prudence. And you'd need temperance, you'd need to look at yourself and be able to say, 'If I go and empty my bank balance, what I'm really doing is indulging to excess my own longing to be virtuous and to discharge my debt.' So I must hold on and think about how my *appetite* to be doing the right thing or to be clearing the slate is involved here and step back a little.

Or, of course, the other way around: I might be asking, 'Is my reluctance to empty my bank balance the result of excessive attachment to my security at the expense of what most needs doing?' And following on from this, given that there will be serious difficulties about treating people *aptly* in many social settings, you need *fortitude*, you need strength to hold to your perception and carry it through.

So, starting with any one of these situations, you can move the pattern round and see how they interlock and how the word you use – 'discernment' – comes in significantly and deeply in relation to all of them.

MZ What you saying, then, is that it's something to do with an *instinct* (I realise that there are various distinctions, philosophical and theological, between instinct and intuition).

RW That's why I'd want to talk about *developed* instincts. It's not just a matter of some natural feeling. There's a cultural element.

MZ   But regardless of which it is, instinct or intuition, there is a sensibility or some such word that enables you to respond aptly at the time in the sense of aptness and justice to *what is happening*. The question is about how you negotiate all of this; and a question that I know people ask is, 'Where does history fit into all of this?' It would seem to me that the answer is to do with *responding*. You're not forgetting history, you're responding to the effects of it.

And so you're responsible for it, which doesn't mean you're *guilty* for it, but that you have responsibility to address the situation – something that Emmanuel Levinas draws out in his reading of Dostoevsky.[3]

RW   It can be another area of huge confusion. I remember in the context of the 2007 commemoration of the abolition of the slave trade a lot of ill-tempered muddle about who should be saying sorry, with people confusing categories left, right and centre. Should we acknowledge that we are heirs and beneficiaries of the terrible behaviour of our ancestors? Yes, without qualification.

Should we *feel* guilt for that, in the way we would feel properly guilty about a deliberate act of oppression by ourselves? That could be theatrical and illusory (possibly an offence against 'temperance' terms of the virtues), and it could trivialise the intensity of the responsibility we should be feeling for things we could actually have done differently in our lives – as we couldn't have made a difference to what our ancestors did. But the question becomes how culture does and doesn't manage to nourish an instinct or intuition towards justice. What stories are being told? What models are being paraded in society?

MZ And what gets repeated? We had a big issue in Australia when our prime minister in 2007 became the first national leader to say sorry to the Indigenous peoples of Australia, which was a massive thing, and different to what you were just talking about. But there are similarities. It was an important symbolic measure; but, in a way, it's not enough, either, because you still have to address the situation, you have to do things about it. It's not enough to say, 'I'm sorry we did that.' You've got to think through what you *are* doing at the same time.

RW And you mustn't then go back home and say, 'Thank goodness I've got that over with.'

MZ That's the issue. That's part of the issue with the 'sorry' in your example: now we can say, 'Well, we're fine now.'

RW And shake hands and forget it.

MZ Because it's an ongoing issue . . .

RW What you'll fail to see is the abiding effect, as you say, of the history which has made people what they are and where they are, which you still have to deal with. Once again, it's a matter of *justice as seeing clearly*. When you've *seen* what history is doing now, whether it's Indigenous peoples in Australia, the descendants of the victims of the slave trade, the person who is living as an adult with the memory of sexual abuse as a child, or whoever, you see what they have been *made* to be and you start from there. You don't say, 'Well, now we've sorted it out . . .'

MZ 'So let's move on.'

RW 'Let's move on.' Fatal words so often.

MZ There's something that's really important in acting aptly and being *present* to the situation in a way that includes history right at that moment. It allows some depth to a situation, and then allows healing to take place at some point in the future. You're not denying the person their suffering, their pain.

RW It's a serious attempt at acknowledging another person's reality, which is what we all hope for. It's something which I remember first coming across in those terms in some of Iris Murdoch's novels: uneven as they can be, they do powerfully present this hunger, this yearning for *being seen justly*. And what she means by this is being seen simply for what we are, seen truthfully – not with the censoriousness that comes from somebody else's agenda of wanting to be in the right, but not with easy indulgence either.

MZ Because that means seeing everything that you are, which includes all the guilty things that you can do, or all the mistakes that you can make ... if I'm getting that correctly.

RW Yes, and I think that's why Iris Murdoch says, 'If God lived anywhere, it would be there' – there at the point where truthful seeing and complex human reality touch.

MZ Do you know in which novel she addresses this idea? Or is it just a theme across all of her stories?

RW There are a couple that come to mind. The phrase I just referred to comes from *An Accidental Man*; but these themes are very much around in *A Fairly Honourable Defeat*,[4] which is one of the most challenging of the novels of her middle period, I think, because what you are shown at the end of that novel is this aspiration apparently doesn't work; there just *isn't* that perspective, except in one or two exceptional moments for unusual people, and yet it is so obviously focal for moral vision.

I talked to her once about that particular novel because it made such an impact on me when I first read it; both that yearning for the *just view* and also the sense that it's perhaps not available. Yet there is in that novel one character – in some ways a very chaotic and floundering character – who seems to see clearly and not to 'mythologise' the people around him. And she said that she saw this character, Tallis, as a 'high incarnation' in the Buddhist sense, someone who has done serious work in dissolving the myth-making, self-serving agency of the ego. At one point, one of the characters says about somebody else that she makes up pictures of people and then persecutes people with the pictures.

MZ That's a very good image.

RW So whatever's going on within Tallis, in the novel, is the opposite of this – which means he sometimes just refuses to get involved in other people's dramas and can't be bothered to take them seriously. People want to pour out their interesting troubles to him, and he is not seduced by curiosity about them. Yet in at least one other instance, he is the only person who can actually take action to change a situation.

MZ I am very much taken by her philosophical work on *The Sovereignty of Good*.[5]

RW   Indeed. Just the same theme comes up there: I'd written an essay on that book as an undergraduate when it first came out, and it was in the light of this that, when I read *A Fairly Honourable Defeat* a couple of years afterwards when it was published, I thought, yes, I see the connection.

MZ   Yes, because *The Sovereignty of Good* suggests that it is in those moments of non-self-serving perceiving that we really understand . . . How does her language there about the Good relate to what we've been saying about virtue?

RW   Well, the Good is a transcendent point of reference for her: it's something that none of us embodies, but it's a point of view we *have* to imagine. We have to believe that there is some perspective from which human beings may be seen adequately and aptly. The Good is whatever would be a comprehensive vision of our being.

MZ   Yes. Which could be described as God's perspective.

RW   'God' very much in inverted commas for Iris Murdoch. But, in the meantime, to have that as a kind of critical, rather Kantian, presence in our minds is one of the things which actively makes a difference to our attitudes to other people. I remember that she uses the example of two members of a family growing into a different relationship – in which the daughter-in-law gradually comes to understand or see her mother-in-law differently.

MZ   I think that the idea that Iris Murdoch is putting forward with that example of the daughter-in-law gradually coming to understand the mother-in-law is about what a 'disposition towards a virtue' would look like – it's not just about the end result, but about a movement towards being a better person. It's perhaps much closer to Hume than to Kant, since, in some ways, it's not based on a categorical imperative, an obligation that must be dutifully discharged, but is a means to invent and create possibilities.

I've been struck, over this last decade, by her writing when I've been thinking through the nature of perception. Her way of addressing the complexity of the Good and ways to express the necessity of it is such an incredible way to move forward the discussion of what is justice. Because the Good is a hard thing to consider and think through.

RW *The Sovereignty of Good* is both a beautifully written and inspiring book, and, in some ways, a tantalising, even confused one. I heard her lecture in Oxford in 1971 or '72; and what she was saying there seemed to be stepping back from the earlier book in some ways. I wasn't surprised when the next couple of novels (including *A Fairly Honourable Defeat*) were much more sceptical, almost despairing. I think she was always wrestling with what imaginable sense it could make to say that there really *was* such a perspective – because if you said that, you were more or less saying you had to suppose that there was a God independent of your own mind; and – at least, most of the time – she saw that as myth and idolatry.

II

Justly Looking

May 2015

MZ Let's return to Iris Murdoch and her argument or idea, both in her philosophy and in her literature, about wanting to be *seen just as you are*. You were quoting her about the notion that if there were to be a God, that's where it or He would be. I want to open that out a bit in a moment, but I want also to talk about Flannery O'Connor because I think her short story 'Everything That Rises Must Converge' is related in some way to this first question about being seen as you are.[1]

RW For Iris Murdoch, it's to do with her novelist's sense that every vision that you and I have of everyone else is bound to be distorted by interest or agenda – by the busy, indulgent ego. We come with this sort of baggage, and therefore we don't see what's there. It's interesting that in the writings of Evagrius of Pontus – one of the great ascetic writers of Eastern Christianity – at the end of the fourth century, he talks about how we can see objects and persons in three different ways. We can see them diabolically, humanly or angelically. The diabolical is purely destructive, consuming: everything is seen in terms of what it can give *me*. The angelic or the divine is seeing things and people as they actually are; but habitually, we don't see like that. Our human seeing is a mixture of the two extremes. So part of what Iris Murdoch is saying is, could we imagine how we would be seen from a point of view that has no agenda, no anxiety, no selfish desire, no rivalry, or whatever else?

MZ   That is very interesting, because that is one way of understanding a kind of literary imagination: wanting to see without all of those vested interests. But coming back to those three different ways of seeing, could you elaborate a bit more about those ways of seeing? Actually, the diabolical is really interesting because we see a lot in those diabolical terms, I think.

RW   Evagrius, like some of the other 'Desert Fathers',[2] doesn't have a crude picture of the devil as just some monstrous external force. He writes that the evil powers manipulate our own natural resources. They shuffle around inside us, as if they're bits of us that we're not aware of or not controlling. And part of what they do is to make us see falsely; that is, to see something simply as it relates to me – how does it serve me? How does it make me secure? – such that everything I see is reduced to that. The diabolical imagination – the diabolical spirit – has absolutely nothing in it except a hungry void inside. That seems to be not a bad definition of the diabolical: being left with no more than a constant, ceaseless effort to annihilate otherness and the other.

MZ   And human perception?

RW   Human perception is an in-between level where we see some things well and some things badly, and where we're still very much concerned to square things in our own terms but are also growing a bit and being challenged a bit. The growth that we're asked to undertake in the spiritual life is the breakthrough to that radically different kind of seeing, which is angelical or divine at the end of the day, seeing things for what they are. God, in this tradition of theology, is the power that simply makes things to *be what they are*. God has no interest to serve. God has no needs to satisfy. Therefore, when God makes what is other, God affirms the other unconditionally. That's it. God doesn't say, 'I wish I hadn't done that', or 'I'm going to make human beings so that I feel happier and have somebody to play with.' That notion has to be swept away completely. And this means that God's perception of the real is utterly without distortion: God saw what he had made and, behold, it was very good. And that takes me right back to Iris Murdoch, who loved to quote what Rilke said about Cézanne: He doesn't paint 'I like it', he paints 'there it is'.

MZ   Yes, this perceptive quality, to 'paint what is there', is almost a revolutionary task for today! I've been going to a lot of galleries recently, and I became fascinated by Monet. There's an exhibition now in London that's called *Inventing Impressionism*.[3] Of all the Impressionists on display, it was his work that I was completely taken by; it feels like he paints 'what it is', what is there. That resonates with what you're saying about Cézanne.

RW   One of the things about Monet and Cézanne, and other artists of that era, is that they go back to painting the same thing over and over again, as a way of saying, 'I know I haven't got it, but there it is.'

MZ   Yes. I'm seeing something new each time. I'm seeing something that may be very subtly different. It's something along those lines, isn't it?

RW   To do justice to what I'm seeing is going to take time and perambulation; I need to walk around it again.

MZ   That's why the paintings last. With painting, you can almost become speechless just looking at it . . . And this immersion in a work is about entering a different kind of time and relationship.

RW   That's right. I'm thinking, too, of the way in which some painters go back repeatedly to the same faces – Rembrandt's self-portraits at different stages of his life, but also Gwen John, one of my favourite artists, painting over and over again the same faces. She was asked by some nuns whom she knew in France to do a portrait of their foundress, Mother Marie Poussepin. There was a seventeenth-century picture surviving – not very good – and they wanted a proper portrait. What Gwen John did was a series of well over a dozen versions: a sort of 'imagining her way in' to Mère Poussepin. They're now in different rooms in the convent. It's the same figure, in different light, slightly different angle, slightly different expression. It's a little like what my sister-in-law has done as a painter: for the last thirty-five years, she's painted her mother literally scores of times.

MZ   That's quite extraordinary. How do you see it when you're looking at those images?

RW   I see a painter trying to do justice precisely to that *there it is* element; never saying, 'All right, I've done that and moving on', but something more like, 'Here's what I see now that will actually make it possible for me to see something different next time. The more I look, the more I see.'

MZ   I also saw some of Turner's work recently. Some of his paintings are chaotic, too – wild; but there's something intense and captivating as well. I think sometimes he had to try and re-imagine things in his studio, so it's a different kind of process; but the effect of seeing – the way he was seeing – is opening up a world, rather than shutting a world down.

RW   Exactly.

MZ   Which, I think, is what you're saying with your sister-in-law painting her mother. It's continually opening up the image, opening up the possibilities in it. Coming back to the literary imagination, remember what you were saying about Murdoch trying to find the point of view where there is no agenda, no personal interest to serve? Not many people can do that, really, can they?

RW   No. In a sense, it's impossible, because you're *always* looking at someone else from another particular standpoint – physically, but also emotionally, spiritually. It's a little like the mathematical idea of an 'asymptotic' progression – always approaching but never getting there. You seek to understand better, as time goes on, the particular ways in which you're misreading, distorting or instrumentalising another. You'll never get to the point where you stop doing it, but you learn to diagnose it a bit more successfully as times goes on.

MZ What about the way Dostoevsky struggles with different points of view in his fictions? Or rather, not 'struggles', but places them so that we somehow have to engage with their diversity along with him. I remember reading *Crime and Punishment* at night-time, before I fell asleep, until I finished it, and it seeped into my unconscious: I'd wake up wretched, feeling whatever was being worked out in his characters.[4]

RW I've often said to people you have to be very careful when you read *Crime and Punishment* – not a good idea to do it late at night or when you've got flu ... But often in Dostoevsky what you have is a pivotal moment where somebody is truly *seen*. Sometimes that's liberating and sometimes it's not. Raskolnikov is, in a way, seen only by Sonya, and Sonya's seeing of him is not sentimental or absolving in an easy way. She wants to make him responsible. In a sense, what she does is commit herself and say, 'When you have admitted your guilt, I will still be there, but I'm not interested if you're not going in that direction', which is quite tough. And in the really chilling chapter of *Devils*,[5] where Stavrogin confesses to Bishop Tikhon his horrific sexual abuse of a child, he is seen – even seen with a degree of compassion and depth – but he isn't able to accept it.

MZ Coming back to justice and courage, this is where human justice would lie, somewhere in this area. We know from the start of *Crime and Punishment* that Raskolnikov has committed the crime. We're not waiting for any disclosure—

RW It's not a whodunnit.

MZ Yes. We know he's guilty. So the question becomes, 'What is the *time* that is needed for someone to work through their responsibility, their wretchedness – whatever it is – their culpability even?'

RW Yes, that's right. To go back to Dostoevsky's *Devils*, and the scene of Stavrogin's confession: Tikhon is the only person who knows this appalling truth, the only one who sees it – and he has a moment of something like prophetic insight with Stavrogin. He says, 'You want to confess this to the whole world, but actually you can't cope with that. What if, instead of being seen as a great melodramatic repentant sinner, people just laugh at you?' Confessing a sin is letting go of any pretence at controlling the image of yourself, and that means you have to imagine not only disgust, but also mockery or even dismissive scorn. It's a very complex chapter. It's as if Tikhon is saying to Stavrogin, 'What you've confessed is something which needs to be seen truthfully, and I shall do that for you, I will see it truthfully, I'll hold it.'

But there are contexts where making this public and talking about it will threaten to destroy, and where your attempts to talk about it will take away even such integrity as you have. Stavrogin wants to make a great gesture of public self-humiliation by telling this story, and Tikhon says, 'Can you cope with how that might work out? Maybe it won't make you feel better. Maybe it'll just leave you feeling humiliated and resentful. Can you bear that?'

Again, this theme of seeing comes up at the start of *Brothers Karamazov*,[6] when Father Zosima prostrates himself before Mitya, the eldest of the three brothers, because he sees something that nobody else sees until very late in the novel. He sees that Mitya is going to be the one who will actually hold the narrative together at the end – this rather rakish, not-very-bright military officer. And Zosima bows down to the ground before him.

MZ There are two things you're saying here. One is to do with the question of how you handle the guilt; the other is about how this relates to seeing and acting justly. You spoke earlier about the character of Tallis in Iris Murdoch's *A Fairly Honourable Defeat*,[7] who is the one you don't think is going to be able to see or act, but he is – which is the unexpectedness of real life, isn't it?

RW I think what Murdoch helps us to get a bit of a fix on is the idea that when you're aware of failure or sin or whatever, what you need is a perspective which can tell you both, 'Yes, you're responsible' and 'No, it's not the end of the world.' Other people's reactions now don't determine everything. You've faced it and somebody else has held the truth of it. Hang on to that; which is so difficult.

MZ We're not trained to do that, are we?

RW We're really not.

MZ Yet it's the only *just* thing, the only thing that can allow people to see each other and allow moments of possibility. How do we create those kinds of moments? 'Virtue' is one way of approaching all this, but I'm wondering whether there are other means.

RW We're supposed to think of Tikhon or Zosima – insofar as they represent the 'holy' in those books – as standing for another 'territory', another and radically different frame of reference. What makes them different is that they're coming to these encounters, as far as humanly possible, without an agenda, without a battle to win. So, the question is, how do we train ourselves to *listen* without battles to win?

MZ So if we return to that question of the just or justice, what we were saying earlier was around the idea of the limits of law, when law is seen as simply some kind of 'settlement'; whereas, this idea of living in justice is something altogether different. We have to try to find those other possibilities. Where do we look? In the cardinal virtues, the theological virtues? Where do we locate those habits that allow what you're talking about?

RW The habit of 'just looking'. *Just Looking* would be a title for a book, wouldn't it?

MZ Yes, it could be this one ... But while we're on the subject of justice, maybe we could talk a little bit about *The Merchant of Venice* and then circle back.[8] I became intrigued by that play because I was interested in the idea of mercy, and there is the great speech from Portia about this. There's something profound being said about mercy in the play and also about *value* – what you value – and how this is played out both comically and tragically in the drama. But does the play actually do it? Watching it recently, I was hopeful, really hopeful, but ...

RW It's a play that leaves you feeling very uneasy – not least because the 'mercy' that Shylock is offered at the end is a rather terrible travesty of justice, in that he is forced to buy his life at the price of his faith. He is forced to deny who he is: the heart of all injustice.

MZ Yes, and it's totally horrible. In the version I saw recently, they show him being baptised, and it's a horror. It's somehow playing him off against what *we* value; playing off his integrity, his spiritual substance against our values and valuing him as nothing. That is what's so disturbing in it – not just the anti-Semitism that some people take away from the play, it's this wider issue that's disturbing.

RW   Part of what's so difficult is the rhetoric at the end of the trial, where all the Christians are in effect saying, 'Look how merciful we are! Look how much nicer we are than you.'

PORTIA

    What mercy can you render him, Antonio?

    . . . .

ANTONIO

    So please my lord the duke and all the court

    To quit the fine for one half of his goods;

    I am content; so he will let me have

    The other half in use, to render it,

    Upon his death, unto the gentleman

    That lately stole his daughter:

    Two things provided more, that, for this favour,

    He presently become a Christian;

    The other, that he do record a gift,

    Here in the court, of all he dies possess'd,

    Unto his son Lorenzo and his daughter.

                  MV 4.1.378–90

So much for 'mercy'. 'What mercy can you show?' That all your money will go to the worthless infidel who has abducted your daughter and caused you the greatest pain that you've known. That pain is so palpable in the play. And on top of that, you must become a Christian, renouncing everything that gives shape and meaning to your life: mercy. And the court applauds.

MZ   So the law is working itself out through its inheritance to the son-in-law, and the faith element has become almost an object that you can toy with. I'm not sure, but there is definitely a split there between the law as it is initially appealed to, mercy as exemplified – so troublingly – by the Christians in the drama, and what would be *nourishing* or *just* in these kinds of circumstances.

RW   'Thou shalt have justice, more than thou desirest', says Portia to Shylock earlier on.[9] More justice than you desire is a very interesting idea; it's not unconnected with the very Shakespearean idea that, if you ask for justice, be aware of what you might get. 'You shall have all justice; you shall have nothing but the penalty.'[10] Think of *Measure for Measure* here as well.

MZ   It is all somehow summed up in the debate about the cutting of the flesh. It's where Shylock's desire for ... it's not even revenge, is it? It's just a weird balancing out of some sort of disorder in his view, which seems monstrous to the other side, and it's played out as monstrous. And so it is; but the way the story is unfolding is that it's the *worth* of that pound of flesh, something to do with the body itself becoming a site for the exchange of value. In the 'merciful' resolution at the end, it's as if the value of his view, his bodily point of view, is not taken into account in that – his pain, his suffering.

RW   He has to surrender the two things that are crucial to him: his daughter and his faith. He's got to surrender himself, but not in a healing or redeeming way. I don't know how you'd play that line, 'Art thou contented, Jew? What dost thou say?' and Shylock's reply, 'I am content'. The only way I can imagine playing it is with an immensely long pause and completely expressionless.

MZ   I think that's what they did in the version I saw. There was that sense of its ridiculousness, if I recall rightly. Certainly, that was the point being made in the way he was baptised at the end. It was kept very, very solemn.

RW   There have been various ways of dealing with it. In some productions, it's made very clear that he's going to go off and kill himself. Laurence Olivier famously – having staggered to his exit – gave an inhuman howl as soon as he was offstage.

MZ   You weren't sure with the production I saw. You just saw Shylock as almost *ghostly* at the end.

RW   It's one of the most heartless endings to any of the plays. You go back immediately to these Venetian aristocrats playing around with each other as if this atrocity hadn't happened. You want to throw them all in the canal by the end. As in *Twelfth Night*, there seem to be no likeable characters in *The Merchant of Venice*.

MZ   So the play doesn't help us with the mercy question.

RW   No, it doesn't.

MZ I'm thinking that if we add mercy to our list of virtues, then it doesn't help us to understand what's involved in truthful seeing. When you were talking earlier about being able to see clearly even one's own crimes, then that does require a kind of mercy, but it isn't the mercy that we're talking about in this play, where everyone seems to have it wrong, Christian and Jew.

RW Yes. Neither Shylock nor Antonio is seeing.

MZ Exactly. Antonio is a bit of a problem character right from the start as well.

RW Yes. The moments when Shakespeare does 'do' mercy in an authentic way are the ones like the scene in *King Lear*, where Lear says, 'Your sisters / Have, as I do remember, done me wrong: / You have some cause, they have not.' And she says, 'No cause, no cause.'[11] That's an absolute clearing of the decks. And in *The Winter's Tale*, at the very end, does Hermione forgive Leontes? We don't really know, because she doesn't say anything. The attendants say, 'She hangs about his neck'[12] and you're left with almost a frozen picture in the middle of the stage, of some wordless, almost desperate, embrace between Leontes and Hermione. Here is Leontes confronted not just with the *memory* of having done someone a terrible injury but the *person* to whom you've done the most unimaginable injury in a fit of real moral madness. There it is. But that 'there it is' can perhaps just embrace and hold something.

MZ It's a bit of what you were saying about Iris Murdoch before. And I think the threads of Murdoch and Dostoevsky are related here. This is a bit of an aside, but not irrelevant: I'm writing a play with my collaborator Christos Tsiolkas and one of the characters – it's a play set in a family context – is the 'stranger' who actually can see the truth of what's going on in a dispute around the father, his care and the family estate. We've been trying to not make the stranger devoid of their own sense of right – not 'right' in the sense of entitlement – but the right alignment to the truth of the situation and the person involved, as we've been discussing. It's about the ideas of justice we've been talking about – how you see justly. And it's interesting having to think how you create that in fiction, because the literary imagination that we're exploring helps us to see these things.

RW   One of the themes of *Lear* is the difference between trying to quantify love or 'worth', or even 'duty', and the actual arising and expression of authentic relation. Lear starts by working with this sort of quantitative model and has to unlearn it in the most shocking and painful way. When Lear meets Cordelia again, he is at first fearful that he will be judged and valued as he has judged and valued others; but what happens is radically different, a real moment of transparency in the drama, in spite of all the horrors that follow it.

MZ   So let's take that back to Flannery O'Connor and the story we mentioned, 'Everything That Rises Must Converge'. The son and the mother go off to the equivalent of a Weight Watchers class. It's the segregated South in the US and you realise that she's profoundly racist, and her son is intensely righteous in his dislike of her. Then she's hit by a black woman when she's trying to give money to her, and then he sees her differently. He realises how vulnerable she is. There's something in her writing which you've written about in terms of grace, which it is. I want to understand that a little bit more. There is an awareness emerging in the son; there's something he hasn't seen, has failed to see and wasn't even willing to see, because he was so eager to see all of the things that his mother was doing wrongly.

RW Quite a few of her stories are really about those sudden moments of seeing. A famous example is, of course, 'A Good Man Is Hard to Find', where the annoying old grandmother at the end looks at the Misfit and says, 'Why you're one of my babies. You're one of my own children!' – a wonderfully O'Connoresque ambiguity, of course.[13] And in 'The Artificial Nigger', the sudden perception of . . . well, what is it? It echoes that phrase of T. S. Eliot's 'some infinitely gentle / Infinitely suffering thing'.[14] They look at this stupid and tawdry figure of a black child, and suddenly . . .

MZ It hits them. In 'A Good Man is Hard to Find', there's something I find really amazing about Flannery O'Connor in the moment you mentioned – the grandmother looking at the killer and saying what she says. It's just so shocking, in a way, that she can say it. The murderers themselves have to be seen as wretched too. She's not trying to *absolve* anybody, but in some way, everybody suffers – and that's why it works. It's not that you identify, but somehow you might begin even to understand the murderers a little, even though you don't really . . .

RW You're invited to feel a kind of pity for them, to sense their tragedy.

MZ Yes, and as far as the actual act of killing is concerned, she allows it to be every bit as horrible as it is. It's what we were talking about before – the space in which the worst can happen, the worst can be done; and it's not acceptable, and it's not tolerable, but how do you manage it, humanly speaking, at the level of relations and the level of how you *tell* such a story?

RW   Part of what makes it horrifying is that the murders take place off stage. The family, one-by-one, are marched away and dispatched in silence, as it were.

MZ   It is one of the chilling things; but it's almost as if we're being told that these are things that happen. People *are* marched off and shot in this impersonal way. In her collection of essays, *Mystery and Manners*,[15] she does say there's a loss of tenderness in the world, and she spells out her sense of what tenderness is, and the connection of tenderness with faith or spirituality. And because of this, you then have a frightening side to tenderness, an obsessive and fearful dimension to it. It can lead to these kinds of atrocious acts because people don't have any sense of how to *work through* certain kinds of virtue, or respond to the suffering of another. In other words, if you only have 'tenderness', there may be a lack of any sense of how to respond justly.

RW   A connection of thought here between Dostoevsky and 'A Good Man is Hard to Find'. There's a moment in Dostoyevsky's *Idiot*,[16] where Nastasya Filippovna says, after her first meeting with Myshkin, 'I've seen a man for the first time'. Now, in Russian, of course, it's just, 'I've seen man', because you don't have definite or indefinite articles in Russian. So what is she saying? 'I've seen a man for the first time'? 'I've seen *humanity* for the first time'? Although Myshkin is a deeply undeveloped character, and one has to recognise that he's *not* a Christ figure in any straightforward sense, part of the way he acts in those early chapters is as a sort of catalyst for discovery or self-recognition.

MZ For others, you mean? Because of his responses to them?

RW Yes, because he's a very undefended person. What he makes possible for others is a kind of unexpected self-recognition. In that connection, he is a vehicle for some kind of goodness, the sort of good man who is hard to find. Though that's only part of what he does and is in the book; he's not an unqualified saint.

MZ I was thinking that the title of 'A Good Man Is Hard to Find' is really interesting because, in fact, good men *are* hard to find – and good women. So it's a truth, in that sense, or even a truism. What I feel in her writing – but also in her reflections on her writing – is that she's trying somehow to talk about wretchedness as much as grace, and she captures what we don't want to admit to ourselves or to each other. She does it comically, as in *Wise Blood*,[17] as much as she does with horror.

RW What she's doing in a lot of the stories, as novelists properly do, is conducting a sort of thought experiment. Let's allow the habitually self-regarding, self-congratulating, self-protecting wheels of our discourse to run on. Then, rather than neatly turning it towards a conclusion, you just have a shot across the bow. You have, almost literally, a stick thrown in the path of the wheels, and there's a great jolt, and sometimes you see something new and sometimes you don't.

So grace, instead of being gentle rain from heaven, can become a sharp kick in the backside from truth. As if something just drops into the situation saying, 'No, it's *not like this*.' And, as in 'Everything That

Rises Must Converge', this leaves at least some people with the thought, 'Have I got this *all* wrong?' Often that's where her stories leave you: 'Have I ever understood anything at all?'

There's a lovely moment in Marilynne Robinson's *Home* – the sequel to *Gilead* – where Glory, the rather harassed, virtuous, homebody daughter, sees the child of the girl that her brother's got pregnant and sees the love and the gentleness of this rather sluttish young girl, and goes away saying something to the effect of 'I understand absolutely nothing'. She's a sort of hardworking Martha figure – a 'deserving' figure. And she sees something which has nothing to do with what's 'deserved'.[18]

MZ   This is where value and worth can't be equated with what *you* believe to be true.

RW   The paradox in 'Everything That Rises Must Converge' is the moment where the old woman thinks, 'Maybe I am a hog'. It's a paradox in that, as she thinks this, you realise that's when her worth – her real value – shines through.

MZ   And it's a very *ordinary* moment, isn't it? That's what's so special about the idea of grace that you're talking about in relation to Flannery O'Connor and, indeed, the idea of grace more generally.[19] Can we call grace a 'virtue' here? Does it become all-embracing of the other virtues?

RW   Grace can become a virtue, or rather, a *habit* in traditional theology; but it's also an event – that spoke in the wheels or shot across the bow – that can at least jolt you out of those habits which are most inimical to *just seeing*. It's that simple, 'No, it *isn't like that*.' And perhaps virtue is, or is born in, the willingness to stay with that, to *sit* with that, as my Buddhist friends would say.

MZ   So virtue can jolt you around a bit?

RW   Surely, one of the things that will throw spokes in the wheels can be somebody's gracious or virtuous act.

MZ   In the same way it can be somebody's *awful* act or the sheer surprisingness of a Murdoch character.

RW   Exactly. There's a scene in a restaurant in *A Fairly Honourable Defeat* where someone is being subjected to racial abuse and violence, and Tallis goes and intervenes, and just smacks the attacker across the face. That's a moment of *grace* in a very odd way, because you're suddenly being shown that 'this is not it', violence doesn't have to happen. There's nothing automatic or necessary about violence and hatred – although it's a violent act when Tallis slaps someone across the face!

MZ   Yes, but it's a surprising act.

RW   It's a surprising act, and it has the effect of grace. You might expect the young attacker to hit back, but he's too surprised and backs off.

MZ   It's a very radical picture of grace here, isn't it?

RW   As I said, it's not grace as just gentle action.

MZ   And it requires a capacity to 'digest' the moment when grace appears.

RW To digest, to back off, to sit and listen.

MZ Yes, and it makes me think of Marilynne Robinson when she reflects, in *The Givenness of Things*,[20] on some of Shakespeare's plays and suggests that 'mercy' is less than grace. Could we say that mercy is tied up with power, whereas grace is more of an invitation?

RW That's very persuasive. Grace has to be something that dawns on me quite outside my sense of my will or capacity, my *achievement* of virtue. I suppose that this is what the Protestant reformers mean by insisting that virtue, even love, won't bring you to the point of real reconciliation because it's still within the bounds of what you, as an individual, think you can do. And grace is just outside this, a moment of 'creation from nothing'.

In the course of this chapter, reference is made to a short story by the American writer Flannery O'Connor, the title of which includes a racially derogatory term. The reference to this work's title does not in any way endorse the attitudes it represents, and is cited only to assist the reader's access to the text.

PART TWO

RECKONING

In this next section, we explore how individual and public languages for justice can embrace both secular and religious sensibilities. During the times that Rowan and I came together, different world events unfolded, from the Syrian refugee crisis, Paris bombings, ISIS attacks, Brexit and US elections to the ongoing economic and humanitarian crises in Greece and other European countries. In the light of these events and our concerns with justice, we discuss the collapsing of human worth and value in a market economies, the role of identity and nationhood in challenging times, and the question of powerlessness in the face of political discontent. We examine the urgent need to consider a form of 'global witnessing' as a response to violence and displacements of peoples around the globe. We discuss how to address the 'wretchedness' in our social histories and within our individual lives, which is also a question of how ethically to respond to the legacies of histories and violence that we have inherited.

Within all of this, we expand approaches to justice through emphasising the importance of learning to live justly, which requires time, patience and discernment. It also involves training the imagination and 'educating emotions' to compel us to live more honestly and truthfully. We consider how loving thy neighbour might essentially involve a friendly generosity and concern, and uprooting one's own sense of privilege to open out the potential for healing and forgiveness. This involves forging new connections and relationships that can nourish and sustain us rather than destroy and separate us.

Some of our reflections here are very ordinary and everyday, but they may be infused with what Simone Weil once considered: that while there is no supernatural cure for suffering, there might be a supernatural use of it. Grace, as we have already suggested in part one, is an invitation to jolt us out of our complicity and it arises from happenstance that might be miraculous and (super)natural or shocking and revelatory. It is this reckoning that may provide us with new visions of justice and the world. In other words, we may be able to learn and 'unlearn' some of our habits of mind and culture through the appeal to the wisdom of grace and attention to reality. This may be our redemption.

III

Reckoning

November 2015

MZ In the last conversation, we were talking about the eruption of violence that can occur between people and you said something like, 'There's nothing automatic or necessary about violence and hatred.' I am thinking about that in relation to our ideas of justice and the just and thinking about what's happening now with the Paris attacks. It's almost like Paris is in a state of emergency. We don't necessarily have to apply it to what's happening now, but we could as well. What do you think about that in relationship to the just and right and so on?

RW Yes, what was in my mind in saying that was that we slip into this automated view of human action. We don't think about finding space for reflection, about the options we have that are not dictated by what's being done to us. We think, 'Something's been done to us.' We must have 'justice', and this means we have to repay in the same coin, or – to use an image I've used before – reply in the same language. What if we recognise that we are free not to?

This doesn't mean a blanket pacifist response. It doesn't mean that force is always wrong. I say that with a heavy heart, but realism demands that we acknowledge that there are circumstances where force of some sort is unavoidable. But it does mean that we don't just have to think, 'Well, they've behaved like bastards to us, so we must behave like bastards to them', which is the machine mentality. That's why I've been struck by what Jesus says on the Sermon on the Mount about turning the other cheek, which is so far from being just a passive moment. It's a really bold changing of the paradigm. You neither hit back nor crumple. You just say, 'All right, carry on, then, if you want to, but I'm not playing that game.' You take an initiative.

MZ What would happen if you did that? It is, in a way, a more courageous act – because the effects of 9/11 are what we're seeing now, the ongoing habitual response to violence. It's as if we are in a constant state of war because of the violent actions and reactions (on both sides) and so that idea of *not acting* is a possible alternative.

RW There's a story from Zimbabwe in the early days after the end of white rule – a tragic enough story, in the light of all that Zimbabwe has endured since then, from the days when Zimbabwe looked like a good-news story. After some upheaval and change of administration, one of the most brutal, murderous, unpopular local bosses is hauled up in front of an impromptu court of village elders. They read him the list of his crimes and atrocities and then say, 'What do you think would be the obvious thing to do in the light of that?' The man says, 'Well, the obvious thing to do is to kill me.'

'Right,' say the village elders. 'Well, that's why we're not going to.'

MZ Well, that's right, and what does that do then? It changes the landscape, doesn't it? I just went to a conference in Zurich and it was called Peace and Reconciliation. One of the speakers there was talking about what's necessary for reconciliation, and one idea he discussed was the need for repentance and forgiveness. The idea of repentance is interesting: it is something about acknowledging a mistake – we were talking about this beforehand with Iris Murdoch. You said if God was anywhere for her, it would be in that imperfection where people are always getting it wrong. I like the idea of repentance – not necessarily the way he (the conference speaker) was using it, but in the sense that there's something necessary in acknowledging and working with imperfection. Would you call it a virtue, or how would you see it?

RW   Yes, I think it's a virtue to the extent that it's a habit of looking at yourself with realism and with self-forgiveness, but also not letting yourself off the hook too readily. Somewhere in that there's a quite complex way of being – being a moral subject of a certain kind. You know it when you see it.

MZ   If you have this idea of repentance that involves the action of turning the other cheek or a courageous act of not 'acting', and acknowledging the mistakes made, then something else has to happen. Whatever we're involved in, in the West, it seems that we acknowledge 'mistakes', but don't really take them on board and then we think, 'OK, the solution will be to continue bombing ...'

RW   As we speak, the House of Commons is debating Syria, and there was a very good cartoon this morning in the *Daily Telegraph* (of all places), which showed the prime minister in a little aeroplane throwing a bomb into a landscape on the ground, where you can see nothing but bomb damage and explosions. The prime minister is saying, 'This'll sort it out.'

MZ   Yes, 'This will sort it out.' There's something quite serious about that cartoon.

RW   It's the addict's last drink. One more bombing campaign and then it'll be OK. I probably mentioned this before, but in the Bible, forgiveness is forward-looking as well as backward-looking. It's actually a matter of establishing relationship, not just acknowledging failure, let alone overlooking failure.

When Jesus gives his disciples the power to forgive sins, he breathes on them and says, 'Receive the Holy Spirit' (John 20:22). In the New Testament, the Holy Spirit is consistently the relationship-builder, the connection-maker. So if you are forgiving, you are making connections, going forward from a state of rupture and separation. To talk about forgiveness in the absence of any of that challenge is really not very interesting. It can just reduce forgiveness to 'Oh, well. We'll say no more about it, then.'

MZ   Well, that's the usual way. That's interesting about the Holy Spirit – because I'm not a theologian, so to think about the Ghost, the Holy Spirit, as connection changes everything. It makes sense, now that I think about it, to see it as a *relation* and forgiveness as establishing new pathways. And I'm thinking the idea of repentance and forgiveness, then, is about honouring your mistakes ...

RW   Yes, honouring your mistakes; and repentance then becomes keeping the door open to a new way of relating. It's not just 'I'm sorry.

Forgive me' and drawing a line, but 'I'm sorry. Where do we go with this?'

MZ Could you imagine that in a diplomatic situation? Seriously, it would be a very interesting adaptation of a negotiating room.

RW Wouldn't it? The problem is that in so many peace negotiations, people are always, it seems, looking backwards and either saying 'Problem? What problem?' or using the deadening bureaucratic pseudo-apology of 'Mistakes were no doubt made, but . . .'

MZ That's the dangerous one, isn't it? Which has nothing to do, I think, with what we're trying to talk to about here. In a way, you have to invent these new relationships. What happens when the other side doesn't hear, for instance? The negotiation with ISIS doesn't seem to be happening at all. Coming to London this time, there was a billboard with a photograph of a guy with a machine gun that said we are practising non-negotiating tactics . . . I found that quite amazing. It is in a public space. It's an image that is readily there and somehow that's acceptable. 'OK, we're not negotiating. We're just going in.'

RW One of the difficulties with a group like ISIS is that there seems to be nothing to negotiate about: as somebody said, 'They have no demands.' Even with al-Qaeda, people would talk about demands, even if they were unrealistic ones like the dissolution of the State of Israel or something, whereas ISIS basically seem to say simply, 'No, no. We actually want to kill you and take over the world', or else, 'We want to provoke the conflict that will lead to the end of the world.'

You don't get very far trying to talk about that; but it doesn't mean you don't find whatever other avenues there are, directly or indirectly, of somehow humanising the people involved in the group, in your imagination.

MZ   I was watching an online programme from Australia because I have been trying to keep in contact with the news there, and there was a young woman, a Muslim activist, who was also pointing out that ISIS have been murdering their own people – in fact, many more.

There's that issue. And the bombing of Syria that is happening now – to prevent death – is going to create more death not only for people in Syria, but also for those who are now fleeing. If we cannot see these relationships, I'm not sure where we are.

RW   There's this popular fantasy that there's some sort of coherent democratic opposition in Syria who will suddenly emerge and turn Syria into Sweden – free nursery schools and milk for children, and paternity leave, which is not really going to happen in a hurry. We were talking about this last night at a dinner at the British Academy; and, interestingly, around that table, with no one particular political axe being ground, I don't think there was one person who supported bombing in Syria. Everyone was saying that the problem is that we have a government and an intelligence service which really don't understand what's going on in the immensely complex political and tribal and religious climate of the Middle East.

MZ   That is interesting, isn't it? Imagine if they did and that there could be other ways to employ intelligence. The parallel happened to me at this Peace and Reconciliation conference. The Paris bombing happened on the Friday night and then on the Saturday there was a panel discussion to try and make sense of what had happened. One was a philosopher from Germany. Another guy was this very interesting pastor and ex-Interior Minister from Latvia. There was a woman scholar who was from South Africa, who was the only one talking sense, and then another theologian philosopher from America, who was talking about understanding 'just war'. All of them except for her said, 'You've got to bomb.' I was quite shocked.

RW Around the table last night, we had the Chief Executive of the Academy, the president of the Religious Studies section of the Academy and his theologian wife, a journalist from the *Evening Standard*, a philosopher from King's College, London, a novelist, the head of a think-tank, a senior priest in the Diocese of London and myself. One hundred per cent against bombing.

Some of the most interesting comments came from the head of the Religious Studies section because although he's a Christian, he's a scholar of Judaism who knows the Middle East well and is deeply familiar with the Jewish world, past and present. He had more authority to comment than most of the rest of us, but we were all saying from our varied experience that the level of knowledge of the situation on the ground within government, and the Foreign Office especially, is now very inadequate. The timescale that people are working to has contracted dramatically. On one level, we recognised that the parameters of what people feel are possible actions have shrunk the choices; but there was still pretty wide consensus about the fact that we haven't, for example, brought the diplomatic pressure to bear we should on Saudi Arabia, which holds the key to a good deal of this.

Again, we haven't learned how to cooperate with the Russians because we've been anxious about our global relations with Russia; not that I hold any brief at all for Putin, but there was a moment when we might have found a common approach to Syria, and it is now lost forever. We have allowed Turkey to get away with a certain amount because of NATO. And we have persisted in the belief that there's a coherent and viable opposition in Syria. However deplorable Assad is, it might have been possible, three years ago, say, to find a way of saying in concert with Russia, 'What would an exit strategy for Assad look like that leaves him with some dignity, and what are the alternatives within the Syrian government and elite that might open the door to change?' Along with a road map towards elections and a plan to mobilise the resources in the Syrian Army as effectively as we can to push back against ISIS, and a concerted strategy to put pressure on Saudi Arabia.

MZ   None of that's happened.

RW   It's easy enough sitting in an armchair in Cambridge to say these things, I realise.

MZ   I know, but – it's still very important to be working with these issues wherever you are located in the world}. . .

RW   I know that some conversations like these have been going on in government and diplomatic circles; but time after time, people seem to have just turned away from anything of this sort, so that a sheerly reactive mindset has dictated options.

MZ   That's where some of this other ethical choice comes in.

RW That's right, yes. The heart of the ethical is something more than the *reactive*. The ethical begins when you are not just reacting.

MZ This is something that came up in our previous conversations. We were talking about how the whole problem with righteous acts or working only according to the law or to the 'just' could be seen in Saint Paul and his theology, in that sense. The 'problem' of being right, feeling right and feeling righteous also becomes part of this discussion, doesn't it?

RW Very much so, yes. Part of what's going on in Parliament today is that we can't bear feeling powerless when we might be righteous. But powerlessness is, in some respects, simply the reality; and if we don't begin by acknowledging that reality, we cannot change it overnight by our own goodwill and effort. This is hard because it means living with not only a sense of powerlessness, but also a sense of a degree of guilt. *We ought to be able to work out what to do and we can't.* That's a very uncomfortable place to be; but it's the only honest place to be.

MZ Yes, I'm trying to find the words ... if you can't do anything, how do you live with that? Of course, guilt doesn't help at all because that leads to even more crimes of a sort because you're trying to repair *without* honesty and *without* truth. I know it doesn't quite capture what I'm trying to say ...

RW No, but I'm with you.

MZ We start from this position, then, of vulnerability, but maybe not even that. There's a lot of the philosophy that I know of ... for example, the work Emmanuel Levinas, and the idea of vulnerability and the acknowledgement of our own and others' vulnerability and so on, which is an important ethical place. But that also doesn't capture what you're saying: starting from a point of not being able to act or even work out anything ... So how do we invent those moments of choice?

RW   There's a kind of transition from the moment of panicked powerlessness – 'I can't do anything' – to something else. The next stage is, 'All right, so you can't do anything; well, sit and breathe, look, listen, and who knows? In half an hour you may discover that there are things that you *can* do, but they're not the things you're frustrated you can't do. You start with frustration: I can't make the big difference. I can't do it all. I'm paralysed.' Then you begin to see that you are actually a limited being; so what, realistically, can you do, starting within those limits, starting now? It can be as modest as you like. Even if you are dealing with this kind of paralysis in a pastoral or therapeutic situation, you might say: 'OK, so can you make yourself your next meal? Can you make a telephone call? Can you send an email?' To somebody in depression and crisis, you might want to say, 'Try this small step. Let's do that.' And you may begin to see that your life slowly emerges from paralysis. Just how that works in international relations, I admit I'm not sure.

MZ   It's harder, isn't it? I am thinking about a good film called *Paradise Now*,[1] which is about Palestinian suicide bombers. It is about their story. It gives the context of who they are and where they are – they come from loving families and all sorts of things that people wouldn't imagine. You're talking about the therapeutic mode of the person, but I wonder what happens in situations where there are no demands given and there is violence.

I wonder what it means to give grace in that sense? Previously, we discussed how grace comes *unexpectedly*; it's not grace coming down from heaven, it comes from a situation in which you would imagine it possibly arising.

RW   There was an excellent piece in the *New Statesman* a couple of weeks ago, in which one of their journalists described an experience in the Middle East, in a crowded street, when suddenly this enormous local man threw himself at the journalist and pinned him against the wall. He thought, 'Oh, this is it.' As he was pressed against the wall, trembling, a large vehicle rushed down the street. The man had been pushing him out of the way of the car. I found that quite a powerful picture.

But I was also remembering a recent British film called *Four Lions*,[2] a very courageous film in its way. The 'four lions' of the title are four Islamic jihadist suicide bombers – a deadly serious topic, yet it's also a comic film. What it does is to show you these four characters in their British Muslim environment. One of them is a very warm, not-very-bright man, a kind father and husband; then there are two completely feckless unmarried young men, and a fanatical and extremely stupid older man. By various means, they all get drawn into the jihadi fantasy, and their incompetence at every stage is monumental. The two youngsters go off to Afghanistan and we're shown them trying to cope with life among guerrilla fighters. They can't work out why they are not praying facing east any longer. At one point, they accidentally fire a rocket and kill the commander of their own terrorist group.

They are all involved in genuine terrorist activity, planning genuine and horrific violence, and they all die. But what we see in the film is a rather poignant story of variously inadequate, muddled people who find excitement and meaning in this. It's a small step towards at least beginning to understand something of the stories of people like this, not to the extent that it instantly makes all the difference, let alone that it makes you feel in any active sense sympathetic to what they are doing, but in that you are invited to feel some compassion for people who are lured into falsehood.

MZ   I think this is the key: *people are people* and it's different habits, different cultures, different ways in which you live that makes you who and what you are, and your belief systems obviously influence that, and so it's the acknowledgement of this difference. And the different ideas of what is right or what is righteous on both sides. That's why I was thinking the Saint Paul ethical point is very interesting: that righteousness doesn't lead you anywhere. It doesn't help in that sense.

RW   'So you're righteous. *So what?*'

MZ   It leads to more damage, more destruction, more violence, when, in fact, it is that point: 'There's nothing automatic or necessary about violence, really' – although we think that somehow humans are naturally violent or aggressive and so on. Well, there's an aggressive part of us, of course, but it's not the one that needs to be cultivated.

RW   No. We have to focus on that *imaginative space* where we can think of other ways to talk and other ways to act, and it's not possible to take that away from human beings.

MZ Which is why films like *Four Lions* or *Paradise Now* open up a space in which to imagine something else or some other truth about a situation which you think is cut and dry. As I was walking here and passing a few people on the railway station, I was thinking, if the government goes to bomb another country, or goes to war, then people aren't going to think too much about it. They'll go, 'Yeah, OK, that's right.' Whereas if there's a different discussion, or story, or image going on and opening out of the imagination, you might stop and think a little bit.

One of the interesting things I've witnessed while making my film *Dogs of Democracy* in Greece is the strikes. There has been strike after strike or commemoration of various things, one after the other, so I went to the general strike when I first arrived. I was incredibly jet lagged, so it was all a bit surreal. It was very peaceful with children and people and music, and it was really trying to say, 'These changes, these reforms, austerity, are killing us.' At one point, there was a stage-managed and orchestrated throwing of petrol bombs, which in itself is a performative act and mode of demonstration, but nevertheless all of a sudden what was a peaceful situation turned into this very, very scary one.

I thought about Gandhi and how violence does not help anything in this context. It was the non-violent part of gathering together that was doing the *work*. I am trying to think about it in the context of today. What we're looking at now is a whole different series of power relations. In Gandhi's experience, there was a clearer oppressor, in a way, even with all of the confusion and all of the difficulties of his day. But the acts of terror that we are seeing now are less manageable. Gandhi's idea of non-violent action still seems really, really important.

Just seeing it live and erupting from an event that was quite lovely to be part of and then this other thing happened just like that. What might these tenets of non-violence mean . . .?

RW   Frankly, I don't know what it means in the Middle East for those who are currently right at the receiving end of it; but I do know what I hear from most of my Christian friends in the Middle East, who say, 'Western bombing is absolutely not going to make life better for us. We will find ways of living with this in our own terms.' Of course, the Christian communities in the Middle East have been forced to adopt what look like passive strategies of survival for a long time. They've not been in a position to dictate terms. They've had to find modes of non-violent co-existence, sometimes at a very high cost.

To go back to last night once again: before the dinner, there was a reception at which a senior Christian cleric from Iraq was present, and I had a conversation with him. He said what all the visitors from the region seem to be saying: 'Just don't do it.'

*

MZ   We started out this conversation with the idea of repentance. The whole undertaking of these conversations is thinking about when *justice fails*, in a way. I'm wondering now whether justice, or the 'just', is a useful term after all. I'm thinking whether the idea of the good or other terms could help?

RW   The problem is, I think, that we've inherited a picture of justice that is a bit mechanical – all about deserving. I should want us to see justice as something a bit more than simply bestowing on people what they are judged to deserve. This takes us back to what we were saying about 'righteousness', and the rather static and patronising picture that entails. If you look at the resonance of the Hebrew word for justice, its roots are to do with 'alignment' – being aligned with, looking in one direction with one another, with reality, with the will of God. In that light, justice is something which is intrinsically very much a matter of activity, the nurturing of a habit of seeing and acting, active – very much something that is in process, rather than just about what's deserved. That's to say, it is something that does not close down but opens up a dimension of our reality.

MZ We raised some of the ideas of alignment in our first conversation together, but I think we were only touching on the idea of alignment. I think there is something important about alignment. Do we still need justice, in a way ...?

RW It's got its uses. The trouble is if you *stop* using it you beg all kinds of questions. When people say about international aid, for instance, that it's not about charity, it's about justice, they have something important to say.

It's perhaps to do with reminding us that there's something involved here that is more robust and less emotional and less to do with doing good to a passive other than what we normally mean by 'charity', and we need to address this as well as talking about love and reconciliation. We need some sense of right relation being restored and allowing what may be a difficult truthfulness to come through – a level of realism. If you abandon the language of justice, you lose this; you lose some of the more necessarily abrasive aspects of restoration or peace-making, which we need for our well-being and honesty. It's very helpful to be reminded that 'caring for the poor' isn't a matter of benevolence from on high; it's a matter of setting things straight, restoring a situation to a proper 'alignment' with reality.

MZ   So it's not a balance of scales. It's about the alignment to the real.

IV

Time and Attention

June 2016

MZ We had previously discussed ideas of justice as an alignment to reality. My concern is how, increasingly, human worth and value seem to collapse into economic imperatives in a market economy. We've seen it in terms of debates around different kinds of nationalisms worldwide and increasingly so in relation to Brexit. How do we think around some of the issues of justice in the context of today?

RW Certainly, one thing that came through in the context of the debate in this country about Europe was a lack of much sense of why our identity mattered, of what we thought was worthwhile, whether on our own or in Europe – a lack of any sense of our moral image and hope for the future. The public discussion was overwhelmingly about security and profit – which, I think, is probably what you are asking about. We bring to this a curious one-dimensionality about our history, as if there is such a thing as a national identity that's eternally fixed and given, not something that we have developed or learned or worked at.

I was listening to a lecture recently about a particular bit of British legal tradition, and how very hard we had to work to get to where we are, how complex it was, and how little we were in fact 'enslaved' to European regulation, as some people were claiming. There is a seriously distorted picture that has become current and it illustrates something that I often find myself reflecting on these days, which is how impatient we are with the process of *learning*.

MZ   I am interested in what you are saying about identity and why it matters, or maybe why *it shouldn't matter*, in a way, and the lack of patience ...

RW   They go together, don't they? If you think there is something about your identity that is fixed and given, rather than seeing identity as something to be shaped and worked at in response to challenges and unexpected circumstances, you will largely ignore the question of what and how you learn. If you do recognise the significance of learning, you can respect the taking of time and acknowledge that there are things that must take their own appropriate time. You become sceptical about the idea that there are given roles that just drop on you, or are there to discover quite independently of your status as a created being living in time and space. This createdness is the one thing that we can't do anything about at all; but beyond that, we are always working with processes, with discoveries.

What bothers me is the passion to reduce everything to the moment of finding an eternally true identity, individual or social or national or whatever. It's a passion that shows itself in various ways, as in all the popular rhetoric about how you can be anything you want to be – as if you have these 'wants' that are just there, and given the right conditions you can simply realise them. But *why* might I want X or Y? Why do I value this rather than that? Why is this worth having? What is possible and what isn't possible for me as inhabiting this place and time? How long will this take? What do I need to be and to do in order to move from here to there?

MZ These are critical questions for us as individuals.

RW Yes, as individuals, as societies and as educators. I came from a conference this morning on children and meditation, a consultation about how to teach meditation in primary schools. I had the experience of listening to school teachers talking about how they encouraged children to be still and open up into silence, to recognise and reflect on their feelings rather than just act them out. And a few weeks ago, I was visiting the school where my daughter teaches. She was helping the children set up a 'prayer garden' in the school yard, and asking what they would expect from a space like this. What would they want to do there? One little boy of about eight or nine said that when he was feeling specially angry or sad, this is where he'd go to look at his feelings. I thought that was spot on.

Often these days, we are sold the assumption that when we have this or that sort of feeling, it is automatically authentic and needs to be acted on. We're all over-reacting to a culture of unhealthy repression, and the assumption can easily be made that the right thing to do is just let feelings run. But the crucial thing is to see that we might be *intelligent* about feelings. David Brooks's book *The Road to Character* brings this into focus a bit. Although the reviews have been a bit mixed (I wrote a slightly mixed review myself), part of what he is arguing there is that what we mean by character is something that is partly formed as a result of people taking *difficulty* seriously. In other words, how do you cope with the fact that you are in a world you can't control? and what do you do with the grit and abrasion of human experience? This needs time and thought, educated feelings. So although I think the book is a bit over-individualistic in some ways, it is making a valuable point on the partnership of thought and feeling in constructing 'character', the sense of a meaningful and coherent self.

MZ There are two things I'd like raise: one is this question of national identity and the other is the idea of grit and character. What is it that we do value? It seems this discussion about Brexit (but not only Brexit) raises this issue of identity and character . . .

RW Some of the language we hear and use seems to say that what we value is just being who we are: we are an island nation, an independent people with a unique affinity to political freedom and so on. But 'we are an island nation' seems to me either false or blindingly obvious. We are in fact several nations making up the British Isles; and, of course, we are not part of the European continent. Being an island explains much about our history but it doesn't, in and of itself, provide any judgement of value. G. K. Chesterton once said that when politicians uttered the slogan 'My country, right or wrong', it was rather like saying, 'My mother, drunk or sober.' In other words, it simply stated a fact of relationship; it didn't tell you what was worth doing or valuing.

MZ It's nothing to do with that idea of sense of time that you were talking about – the need for time and patience around these matters.

RW There's something of a paradox here. Some politicians and commentators are very concerned that we need to know something about our national history. And for those who use that language, the stress is often on knowing the history of our imperial adventures, our great victories, perhaps our pioneering democratic institutions. And I think, yes: we ought to know about our history, we ought to know that where the United Kingdom ended up historically is and was rather surprising. We had to work at becoming this kind of society, and we experienced advances and reverses. For example, we had one civil war so traumatic that it put us off the idea forever, but one of its lasting deposits was a very strong conviction about the rule of law and about the subjection of the monarch to the law. So the historical lesson is that we make these advances because of various events, including deep conflicts; it wasn't easy and obvious. So the importance of teaching our history is that it shows the process by which we became who we are: it's not just a record of natural superiority and wisdom.

MZ If we think of the UK or Europe or the US, or whatever country, the quest for national identity seems almost absurd, or certainly strange, as the making of our societies has always, to a large extent, been based on migration. That's the reality. When you were talking about *difficulty* and processing of *character*, it seems that human value involves questions of how we should live or how we should progress and how these different elements make up our identities. In some ways, we have to learn how to be hospitable – even with all the difficulties that involves – and I think this also relates to ideas of charity and justice, as we have previously discussed, the idea of *seeing wholly* the context of our relationships.

RW   Yes. That's a point about the fact that the global stranger is not on the other side of the world. Of course, the current phenomena of migration are practically challenging in some contexts; but are they intrinsically more difficult than experiences we have had in the past? We can easily become fixated on this myth of national or cultural identities that are necessarily opposed to each other, and it's a very dangerous one.

I say that not in the least to commend a kind of rootless airport cosmopolitanism; we absolutely need to know our past and to have roots in some sort of story and location. I am very self-conscious about being Welsh and very gratefully aware of being connected with my Welsh heritage, of having a Welsh identity, and I make no bones about it. But I don't for the life of me see why that should mean that I must then go around saying or implying that being Welsh is the best way of being human and that all other ways of being human are somehow defective. That's where I turn to theology, to Saint Paul's notion in I Corinthians that whatever gift we are given is given *so as to be given again*.

Think, then, of British history, with its particular concerns about law, *habeas corpus* and jury trial, all of those liberties that the executive power can't just overrule, all those take-for-granted ordinary civil liberties. They have taken a while to discover and consolidate, and we have often exported them to some other societies, with varying success; but, at best, we have seen them as gifts to be shared, not simply as affirming our miraculous superior wisdom as British. In a much more informal and impressionistic way, the fact that Wales has an unusual literary and musical heritage is something I am happy to share and communicate to others.

MZ   Sharing, in a way, is what you are talking about ... which is another way of thinking about our relationships and social bonds, how we can encourage a richer sense of our identities and experience.

RW   It's the notion that whatever identity is *given* is something which potentially enriches not just me but my neighbour. I think the notion of 'identities which enrich my neighbour' is the breakthrough point.

MZ   Yes. It stops you thinking about yourself, it's something about that connection or sense of the gift that you are talking about. It's not a demand in the usual sense. It's the relational aspect of our human responsibility, which is a different kind of socio-political philosophy (much of our political thinking is about 'demand'). It also enables a sense of communion, of coming together ...

RW   I have been re-reading some of Bonhoeffer's *Ethics* in the last few weeks,[1] as I have to lecture on the text. Some of what he is arguing there is to do with this point. Of course, he is writing in a very particular political situation, where he is up against a mythology of national identity, which is about as repressive, unchallengeable and generally hostile to the other as it could possibly be. But, sometimes rather obliquely, he stages a confrontation between this mythology and what is implied by the way in which we understand the identity of Christ as the supreme instantiation of the human – an identity that is entirely defined by existence for the other.

The power and the depth of Christ's being there is that he is there for the healing or the absolution of the neighbour. So if the church lives in the 'territory' defined by Christ's identity, this is how the church must live. It can never rightly be in the business of policing its own borders against rivals; it can't be constantly on the defensive. Bonhoeffer himself had, of course, been part of the (pretty limited) church resistance to the Third Reich; but later he distanced himself, in a way, saying that the trouble was that in resisting Hitler, the resistance party, the 'Confessing Church' had become caught in a self-regarding posture, failing to see who was suffering most deeply and to ask how the wider situation could be changed. We can't just ask for a 'native reservation' where we're left alone; but most of us will fight quite hard to be left alone. Bonhoeffer says that is entirely the wrong way around.

MZ   It's a little bit like now, isn't it?

RW   You could say that.

MZ   In that sense of Europe and the UK—

RW   We have fought to be left alone—

MZ   Yes. And so how do you start to understand that you are connected anyway. What does it mean for the process of learning and that sense of moral image and value?

RW   I don't think, in the long run, you can talk much about 'value' unless you have that sense of the mysteriousness, the dignity, the claim of the stranger; otherwise, your value just becomes a large flattering mirror for your preferences and prejudices – 'This is what I like and what I think is worthwhile.' What someone like Bonhoeffer is focusing on, in contrast, is the sense of worthwhileness, the value that emerges when you are being knocked off centre by the reality of the other, by what the other does and how the other affects you. In a way, it's 'Theological Ethics 101', but it doesn't hurt to rehearse this sometimes.

MZ Yes, we can't get very far in terms of human value and worth, in that sense, without addressing the stranger. What are the ways of cultivating that value? We often think about value as tied to objects and money and profit. I think the nicest moments between people are the things that happen unexpectedly and that you can't anticipate . . .

RW You can't anticipate or purchase.

MZ We live in our everydayness and we also live in the sphere which is the 'nation'. How do we work these relations of value together? In other words, how do we move forward without destroying ourselves?

RW It's a serious point, given that we are in the middle of what seems to be a global spiral of paranoia and rising violence of various sorts which, even twenty years ago, we wouldn't have predicted.

MZ When we met last time, the Paris bombings had just happened, and that was only six months ago. It's been unimaginable some of the things that have recently occurred.

RW That's right. As you say, we can pay lip service to these ideals of reciprocity and respect in our individual lives and yet so much of our public life still seems predicated on the obviousness or inevitability of violence and reprisal. I keep coming back to the priority of education – but the education of emotions and imagination. Education, as so often discussed today, is seen as the transfer of information and skills so that we can become effective cogs in a productive wheel. But it doesn't have to be like this.

We had a visit in college recently from a school in East London, students who were coming to have a look round the university to be encouraged to think that university wouldn't kill them; but they did something very important for us as well. In school, they had been studying Shakespeare's *Macbeth* and developing variations on themes from the play.[2] These were thirteen-to-fourteen-year-olds, and they'd devised what was in effect a twenty-minute dramatic meditation on the play, highlighting certain words, rhythms, images and themes. And I thought that if you are a thirteen-year-old girl from a Muslim family in Tower Hamlets in London engaging with a text like *Macbeth*, squeezing the pith out of it, you are really learning, really moving out of your comfort zone and discovering new thoughts and feelings, but also learning new ways of seeing the humanity you share with others – just as, of course, a thirteen- or fourteen-year-old girl or boy from a white British family engaging with some classic text from the Muslim world or some other culturally distant setting would be taken out of their depth in constructive ways and begin to learn new things.

MZ   That is what we need. If we can talk a little bit more about inhabiting the space of the other and what that implies, the *Macbeth* example is a good one, and I do wonder about a white kid engaging with a classic Muslim text. It seems to me to be very much about giving up 'identity' and learning about 'communion' – in that very real way of occupying the same space and sharing experiences, human to human, and, in some ways, human to non-human as well. Personally, I love very much the *Conference of the Birds* by the poet Farid ud-Din Attar,[3] which is an allegorical reworking of the Islamic doctrine of Sufism and explores the tensions of identity, value and worth.

RW Sometimes people get anxious about this sort of thing as if recognising the riches and the challenge of culturally different sources were somehow to rubbish the resources of our own culture. We've been going through a great debate in our universities about 'decolonising' the curriculum, and many think this is a kind of treachery to our heritage, fuelled by political correctness. We need some common sense here. What makes the classics of our own tradition worth holding on to and returning to is precisely that they continue to generate new and unexpected insight. They may have been – they have been – used at times to support racial or class agendas, they may themselves be marked by assumptions and convictions we don't share or even want to repudiate; but they have something that goes on nourishing and stimulating. We can recognise the shadows in our history without just blanking it all out; and so we can also recognise the new perspectives and provocations of other cultures and faiths and literatures without thinking that this commits us to tearing up all we have learned in our own cultural world.

MZ Yes. I think there is a need to seriously challenge our cultural habits, and at the same time, to take *responsibility* for previous historical actions without denying them. I think this paves the way for a better understanding of our histories in the present and the potential for creative learning and imagination.

RW So we really need an 'empathetic' educational philosophy where we have opportunity to inhabit other worlds in an environment that is safe enough to do that. And this is where some of the problems arise: people worry whether they are safe enough. Some of the anxieties about national identity and British values seem to arise because they don't know who they are or where they are and they clutch at what are often very unreal versions of these historic identities. A really solid cultural environment should be able to say, 'Yes, by all means go and experience something else, feel its texture and feed it back into our own world.' I am certainly not complaining about technological and scientific education, but I would want us to understand the imaginative and creative side of this as well. I'd love to see science taught in a way that brought out its imaginative richness, its creative and risky elements and even its linguistic adventurousness – all those extraordinary metaphors in physics and cosmology!

MZ   Absolutely. I think the ideas of safety, feeling safe, and trust are essential in both personal and political spheres. Many years ago in the Australian political environment, trust was bandied around: whom could you trust, which politician could you trust? At the moment with Brexit, nobody seems to believe anyone. I don't think uncertainty per se is such a bad thing, but it's a problem when *uncertainty* is built on lies and this becomes the so-called reality.

RW   It generates a real cynicism about public life and a pervasive sense of being betrayed – something I hear quite often from my son and his friends, or from my students. Betrayal – and sometimes also the sense of being treated with contempt. 'Don't they realise we can see they are lying?' The major casualty in this process is the credibility of people in public life.

MZ   I think that lack of credibility was already there. This situation has made it worse. I wonder about the importance of a sense of mysticism, or a sense of imagination in relation to our values and identities – the ability to recognise the uniqueness of others and ourselves, and at the same time to create a sense of safety in and around public discourse. In a way, we can talk about it as individuals, but we inhabit realms that are both public and private; we live in a world where we interact with each other and we have a responsibility for that.

RW   And also where those interactions are not entirely shaped by us, so we can be wrong-footed and disadvantaged in the process. There is no quick route to a political solution. And yet, all that being said, there are contexts we can work at, there are international networks we can work at, which foster trust. I suppose one of the reasons for the fact that I still believe in the church is that it can be one of those institutions we can trust; because, ideally, it is not there just to fight its own cause, it can build these cross-cultural relations without a hegemonic or oppressive and alien agenda.

I think of people in parishes in Somerset or Yorkshire going off to spend a fortnight in Zambia or Tanzania to help dig a well or train a midwife or something like that. It's as significant as any United Nations resolution. We need more and more of those opportunities. Of course, there's the risk we are so often made aware of these days, the 'white saviour' mentality; but most of those who engage at first hand are overwhelmed by what they receive, not by what they achieve. That's another aspect of empathy, overused as the word is: the sheer capacity to inhabit a stranger's perspective, even momentarily, and to know that it changes you.

MZ   I often worry about the word 'empathy', as it has a sense that you have to inhabit that place somehow, and I think that it's not empathy, actually, it's something else. It's beyond empathy, in a sense... You can't really inhabit someone else's suffering, you need imagination—

RW   You remain yourself, and that's where imagination comes in. I think the reason why I share these reservations about the word 'empathy' is that it can suggest a sentimental 'yes, I know' reaction—

MZ   Yes, which then leads to a whole range of problems.

RW   From time to time, I've said to people, especially in pastoral ministry, 'Sometimes the most important thing you can say to someone is not "Oh I understand", but "I have no idea what you are talking about – because you are *you* and I respect that".

MZ   Coming back to character and the book you mentioned, shouldn't the point be that *I don't understand*, and that this should be the opening for a dialogue?

RW   Saying, 'I don't understand, please tell me. Have we both got time for this?' There are two ways of getting dialogue wrong: 'I don't understand, so go away and don't bother me' and 'I *do* understand, so go away and don't bother me'! Both amount to the same thing, the same refusal to learn.

MZ   This is about the importance of the *time it takes to learn something*. And this seems to me to be about a process of justice – in other words, to really 'see' and recognise the experience of others and ourselves in the process.

RW   We are back to the theme of valuing the process of learning.

MZ   Valuing the process of *unlearning*, too.

RW   Interesting that this was a word that came up this morning in discussion with some of the school teachers: they said that doing meditation with small children can be, for *adults*, a very important experience of unlearning. It's quite risky. You are losing some of your all-important control over the children. It's no small thing.

MZ   Yes, to give away authority, in that sense, shows respect towards children, which they can feel, and which allows the *unexpected* to flourish between adults and children in that kind of environment. It's definitely worth taking the risk!

RW   Tying all this in, again, with our recurring theme of justice, I think something is fleshed out here in respect to justice: 'doing justice' for or to another person is the willingness to take some of those risks, to give some of that time.

MZ   Absolutely. Taking risks and giving time: I am also thinking about the idea of the 'democratic', and the need to be more democratic and to have a more open process. How might that relate to our ideas of justice?

RW   Indeed. I think one of the difficulties with our use of the word 'democratic' is that we sometimes assume it essentially means no more than mass popular opinion – which is why a referendum or a plebiscite can seem attractive as the obvious way of expressing democratic freedoms. It's not 'mediated': I can say what I think and what I want, and that is it. The trouble is that you can only configure this in terms of simple binary choices – which won't tell you very much about the processes of implementing and living with choices. What I believe that proper *representative* democracy does is two things. First, it engages and respects your intelligence more fully than a plebiscite. It says, 'Now you are voting for a person and setting up a relationship with them in which they are answerable to you; this is important, but being answerable to you doesn't mean that you control them, and that's equally important. It is up to you to sustain the kind of engagement with them that will repeatedly cement confidence and trust.' That is one very important aspect of representative democracy, and the other is that it challenges the tyranny of the majority. A proper representative democracy says that *everybody* needs representation, everyone's voice needs to be, as it were, finessed into the public discussion. The world doesn't divide into winners and losers; every voice still has a right to be heard.

MZ   Without fear.

RW   Without fear. After the vote last week, there were those who said, 'Britain has spoken.' Well, as part of the 48 per cent whose views didn't prevail, I'm not very happy with such a formulation. If Britain has spoken, it has said two very different things in almost equal measure. And there's the problem: a plain majority isn't the end of the story. That is why we have to reflect very carefully on what we mean by democracy and not assume that it reduces to popular votes on a series of yes-and-no questions. Most of the questions that have to be dealt with in the national forum are complicated. We are complex societies, our relations with one another are diverse, the realities that confront us are very challenging; so we try to find people whose intelligence we rely on, whose openness for discussion we rely on, whose integrity we rely on, to pursue that conversation.

It's interesting to go back again to Bonhoeffer, who said in a letter in the late 1930s that if ever Germany got beyond Hitler, the last thing that should happen should be any kind of plebiscite, because Hitler came to power by plebiscite; even a conventional democratic election might not be right, because something had gone so radically wrong with the democratic imagination. We are going, he said, to need a period where – abnormally but necessarily – there has got to be some political moratorium in which we can recover a sense of what representative democracy is about. Quite a challenge.

MZ It's a challenge because of what democracy now means in Europe and the US, and the 'problems' that have occurred in the name of democracy. In the context of Europe and the Greek crisis, there has been a very strong feeling that undemocratic processes have prevailed, whereas, paradoxically, we can say that Britain has had a 'democratic voice', and here it's fallen short on all levels, as you have pointed out. With such an amalgamation of countries, the question of justice becomes even more skewed.

RW Very skewed. Yes. If justice genuinely is justice for all, then the simple winners-and-losers game in politics is going to be unjust. We are going to need more than the binary choice to secure something like this. So once again, we face the question of how we work in a genuinely representative system.

MZ It's quite amazing that each time I see you there's major events happening around the world. I think you are right in saying none of these issues have been unprecedented. The friends I am staying with in London feel like the issues around Brexit and the political machinations are as big as the Second World War in terms of economic and political fallout. My concern is the deterioration of relationships between people and the lack of generosity.

RW Lack of generosity – yes. So many people have commented on the sourness and venom of the debate and that doesn't all go very well.

MZ What we haven't touched on, but if can we pick up on now or later, are certain issues around racism that have emerged.

RW And, of course, the referendum attracted a whole cluster of anxieties about race and strangers, which had nothing to do with Europe, so became a kind of displacement.

MZ Yes, it is interesting and it is a displacement for a whole range of things that people can't fathom.

RW The example I used, writing in the *New Statesman* a couple of weeks ago, was the closure of a steel works in South Wales. It was a decision taken by an international Indian-based conglomerate, Tata, and had nothing to do with Europe; but it connected immediately with the fact that so much of the population of industrial South Wales has been living with a sense of utter lack of control for so long; and many, therefore, will have voted to leave because of this deep and hurtful sense of having yielded control, intensified by this latest development. But what they yielded control to wasn't Europe so much as globalised economy; and if you want to unscramble the global economy, well, there's a lot to be said for that, but this is not necessarily the way to go about it.

MZ No, absolutely not. And I'd like to consider again the issue of generosity of mind and spirit here and how that might apply in both a practical and conceptual sense to individual and public life. If we return to our earlier conversation on charity, I wonder whether charity is part of this process of justice, and the time it takes to 'unlearn' cultural habits. I recently read some interesting thoughts on the topic by Emmanuel Levinas, where he says: 'There is a possible harmony between ethics and the state. The just state will come from just men and just women and saints rather than from propaganda and preaching . . . that charity is impossible without justice and that justice is warped without charity.'[4]

RW The essential connection is in what Simone Weil calls 'attention'. Both justice and love depend on a sustained paying attention to what is there before you, putting aside your own agenda, your own preoccupations or fears or preferences and seeking to see clearly. Generosity begins not in the overflow of warm feeling, but in a patient looking and listening. It's why love needs contemplation; why the Buddhist, as well as the Christian, tradition lays such stress on compassion being the fruit of 'dispassion' – which is absolutely not chilly detachment, but a freedom from your own feverish desires when you look at another. And it's certainly true that lasting social justice comes when habits like this are engrained in a society, not just when laws are passed. Trying to change behaviour by law without deepening the cultural resource people are able to draw on is a recipe for resentment and failure. Hence, the priority of an education that seriously looks towards educating emotion.

V

Witnessing

January 2017

MZ   For today, I want to start with a line from a Leonard Cohen song where he reflects on the state of the world, and he says something like we were broken, but now we're borderline. I feel that is where we are right now in a political sense. It's very interesting times, broken as we are, but now we are at a crucial stage.

RW   Well, it does feel globally as if things have reeled backwards in the last couple of years. As if certain kinds of hope have become less likely – the hope that we can get coordinated international action on various things, that we can get a shared solution to the refugee challenge, let alone the climate challenge. It's as if all over the political map, people are saying, 'That's just not realistic; all we can do now is simply look after our own and keep our fingers crossed.' The disconnection that most worries me is people's failure to see how all these major crises are interconnected – that there's a role played by environmental crisis in political instability, for example. The Middle Eastern political situation is shaped, in part, by environmental climate issues in the form of water shortage. In certain African contexts, issues around the environment similarly drive political crisis, as traditional patterns of pastoral life and cultivation are threatened; and political unrest and violence, involving wholesale displacement of populations (as in South Sudan, for example) intensifies the environmental problem in a vicious circle. As I find myself saying again and again, crises don't read maps, they don't stop at national boundaries.

We have had a chance to get things together, and we still have some instruments we ought to be able to use. The Paris climate accord (Paris Agreement Under the United Nations Framework Convention on Climate Change) looked like a step in the right direction, even if woefully inadequate in many others. We did have very briefly (though it's hard to remember it now) something of a coordinated European approach on migrants and refugees, at least some shared protocols. Pretty much all of this we have now simply given up on. And it's not as if we can simply say, 'All right, we are now focusing on guaranteed security within the nation-state'; these major problems arise because, as I've said, great national and geo-political issues don't respect nation-state boundaries, and also because the nation-state itself has already been weakened by economic globalisation.

MZ   At the moment, I think that's the challenge. I'm interested in this 'failure of hope' – because, in my view, we look towards hope in a negative way, or at least the wrong way around: we look for hope in grand things, rather than small structural things and I'm interested in these kinds of dimensions. How do we cut across this global challenge at national and local levels? Paradoxically, we have this current situation of the closing down of the nation-state, and the result is a new kind of nation-building or nationalism. How do we open it up again to create hopes that are more sustainable, in a way, or real?

RW We're probably entering a period where global solutions to global problems will become less likely, unfortunately. We can only hope for a kind of *global witness* – a network of global witness in very diverse contexts, where people can show that some other kinds of relationship are still possible. And this, to my mind, is where religious institutions and communities become important, and academic institutions as well. We also need to be working with the strong awareness in the under-thirty-five generation that a closed or self-sufficient national identity is something you have to take for granted.

MZ They don't accept the rigidness of national boundaries. Is that what you are saying?

RW I don't think they do; the bare fact of the levels of international travel that a lot of young people take for granted now, this strikes me very strongly when I look at my children's generation. They assume a freedom of movement around the globe, which my generation didn't, outside a very small and very privileged minority. This is one of the reasons that generation finds Brexit so hard to understand. Many of them feel a huge moral indignation about it, but even those who don't feel moral indignation feel a kind of bafflement, as if what they've assumed is being taken away, and somebody else's definition of national belonging and the possibilities of international relation has taken over.

There's also a great deal of work also to be done (and I've written a bit about this in the last few months) on the importance of small-scale political action: how do you think carefully, morally, strategically through local politics, local challenges, so that people at that level have a sense of agency restored to them? – because the force and energy of 'populism' has so much to do with the feeling that agency has been lost, and people will respond warmly to anything that seems to offer a greater capacity to make a difference. What then matters is how you learn to tell the difference between something that genuinely gives you a freedom to affect things in your environment and a purely cosmetic set of offers, a rhetoric of liberation and control that doesn't change underlying patterns of power.

MZ I am interested in what you are saying about witnessing – witnessing that involves different kinds of relationships, and how agency can be given back to people. How does this witnessing work and what sort of attitudes do we need?

RW I was very struck, when the first child refugees from Calais started arriving in this country, by people – especially from the local churches – turning out on the streets with placards saying, 'You are welcome here' – saying, in effect, 'We don't really care about the posturings at high level, or the policy complications, or the angst about numbers. We just want to let *you*, this particular person in need, know that you are welcome with us.' It doesn't answer policy questions at the macro level, but it does show that something unexpected and generous is possible.

MZ It shows the humanity.

RW   It shows what quite a number of factors might lead us to conclude – that when faced with human need and human destitution at close quarters, most people in this country are instinctively open in their response.

MZ   I've witnessed this over the last years, and how people will generally respond if somebody falls over on the street. Recently, I was in Barcelona and a young man jumped off a building in a suicide attempt. It was terrible, but all of a sudden, people came to help – or course there were 'onlookers', but there was a genuine response. There is something about proximity.

RW   Yes. Somebody reading about migrants in the right-wing press would be given a certain picture of how much there was to be afraid of, and yet they'd be really rather shocked if the attitudes expressed there were to be embodied locally towards somebody they'd actually seen or encountered first hand.

A memory from my days in Canterbury is of talking to some people who worked with detainees in the Dover holding centre, where migrants were detained before being deported; some of these volunteers would go to local schools to talk about the issue and were able simply to test out with young people: what do you think is going on? Who do you think these people are? What do you think is the scale of migration? What are the numbers? They would talk to them directly about these issues and invite them to think about them in relation to actual flesh and blood individuals that they could meet. It made a difference.

And that relates, in some way, to the paradoxes around electronic communication and social media and all the rest of it. On the one hand, we have this extraordinary communication tool that crosses boundaries and crosses cultures. On the other hand, as somebody said a long time ago, 'A lie is halfway around the world while truth is still putting its boots on';[1] and without some contact with somebody whose perception you have good reason to trust face-to-face, you won't break through the propaganda and the stories that suit you, the prison of the echo chamber.

MZ   At the moment, I am working on a documentary on music and migration and trying to think through proximity;[2] I am trying to bridge that gap through music and the experience of refugees and migrants across generations. I have found that when you are with people who experience forced migration, it's saddening, it's real. Yet the way we understand it is so separate from that reality. I think witnessing involves some kind of respect for people and situations, but how do we close those gaps, or rather, make it possible to 'witness' others?

RW   Respect is a good word. But it also goes with something almost more basic, more prosaic, which is a kind of *friendly curiosity* about other people; sometimes 'respect' comes down with a rather heavy weight. The sheer willingness to *find out* is what I mean by friendly curiosity, and for that to happen, of course, people do need to have a reasonably secure environment for it.

You can't just force it and you can't make it happen by aggression or bullying. It's true enough, sadly, that people have talked about pro-Brexit voters or pro-Trump voters in aggressive and contemptuous ways; but it won't do to talk in such terms. You hear it and you know it is absolutely not good enough. These are not fools or villains. Even if you disagree powerfully with the judgements they make, to get anywhere you have to assume that they have reasons; that they have, to some extent, thought and felt this through; that they have a story to tell about how they came to think and feel these things. If they're to move on, then that thought and that feeling has to be taken further.

MZ So that friendly curiosity acts both ways . . .

RW It does. After all, why should they be curious about you?

MZ It would seem it opens up a space for the possibility of understanding.

RW I hope so. And this really makes it all the more urgent to ask: Where do we in our society have those spaces? How much does our educational system open that up – right through to tertiary education, not just in schools? In the period leading up to recent general elections in this country, sometimes churches and other religious bodies were the only institutions able to get candidates from major politically parties physically into the same place to answer questions face-to-face; how we do that and what spaces we provide are crucial.

Last week, I was in one of our local prisons for a few hours with a group, talking through some fairly large questions about the good life and the good society, and I thought, it's a bit worrying if we have to go into prison to have these conversations. Yet it was indeed there that we had a very direct and unmediated exchange and disagreement about very important topics.

MZ Can you give an example?

RW   People disagreeing quite strongly about some of the issues
we've already talked about, Brexit or Trump – and, of course, they
have their own views about how the justice system works in this
country, as you can imagine; but it was that unvarnished quality
of debate with people, people who are not walking away
immediately.

MZ   Yes, and having to confront it, in a way.

RW   It all seemed a very good model. As I say, if we have to go into
a prison to find it, we're not giving enough breathing space to thoughts
about our social fabric.

MZ   I know we've talked about blame before, but there's something
about blame, forgiveness and mercy that we require now more than
ever.

RW   Yes, there's a kind of pathology today in some cultures and
public discourses, which assumes that if you admit failure or
wrongdoing in your collective past, you are emptying your bank
account, so to speak; so you can't admit anything. You can't admit, say,
that the last president but one was a corrupt and abusive criminal. You
can't admit that your last government but three or four was complicit
in genocide.

It's a kind of transcription, into collective terms, of a very honour-
preoccupied society where you can never afford to lose face, and it's
very strange and troubling. Look at a context like the Balkans: bluntly,
every national group in the Balkans seems at some point or another to
have done unspeakable things to every other national group. Nobody
is *just* a victim. Nobody is *just* an aggressor. People need to get to the

point of saying, 'I'm a victim *here*, but I'm an aggressor *here*; *we* are victims here, we are aggressors here.' That's the truthful historical perspective, and we somehow have to see what might be possible if we resolve together to be neither victim nor aggressor. That's quite a challenge; and at the moment, with a particular type of nationalist ethos and rhetoric steadily mounting, it's becoming less, rather than more, likely.

MZ   Yes, that is particularly true: how do you see yourself as both the one that has caused the harm and the one who experiences the harm, and, in other words, having to admit your mistakes and not blaming the other group or the other person?

RW   To state the obvious, the analogy is with how we grow up as individuals. Other people genuinely do bad things to us. We are, most of us, in some respects, victims. And we genuinely do, consciously or not, hurtful and damaging things to others. To deny either of these is very dangerous. If we deny that bad things are done to us, we deny ourselves the tools for understanding what made us who we are. We absorb guilt into ourselves. We take on the tragic load of abuse and violence, and we internalise that violence and so destroy ourselves. We implode morally and emotionally; you'll see this again and again in the lives of individuals who live in denial or suppression of what has been violently taken from them.

Equally, if we refuse to accept that we are also capable of damaging others, then, instead of internalising it all, the violence is pushed out. It's loaded onto others and I go through life wondering why it is that I'm constantly in conflict with everyone, and never saying, 'What's the role I've played in this?'

Somehow, to get into that place where you can face both your failure and your suffering, or loss without a kind of self-loathing, that's a lifetime's job. We know that this is crucial for the well-being of a person. We are usually a lot less clear that it's part of the well-being of a society as well.

MZ   Yes, that's right, having to think at that scale.

RW   It is hard when our culture insistently celebrates some questionable things or canonises ambiguous aspects of our history – as with the century-old struggle over the history of the British Empire. You have the painfully uncritical imperialism of so many in the pre-First World War era, and you have the most fanatical hostility to empire later on. At some point, you have to come around to saying, 'Well, it was something we *did*, and it was an odd mixture of idealism and mythology, self-interest and violence, and some of it was indeed terrible. Some of it was perhaps better than some of the alternatives; but we don't have to believe that it was a flawless exercise in universal benevolence any more than we have to believe that it was a completely cynical exercise in mass selfishness.'

MZ   In colonialism, yes, that's interesting. Having to address with a certain realism and also a certain understanding to work *with* rather than against the past.

RW   Looking at history, we properly make moral judgements; but, like the judgements we ought to make about ourselves, they mustn't be panicked into a false simplicity.

MZ I am thinking of your book *Christ on Trial*, and one of your most recent books *The Tragic Imagination*,[3] and how both shed light on that scale of understanding – how we are implicated, and the tragedy, but also the imagination necessary. So if we address how we are implicated and if we do understand that, then there is the possibility of mercy and forgiveness. I think this possibility might provide a different temporal experience and temperance in relationship to understanding.

RW Yes, I think that's exactly right that this is connected to mercy. If I am, in every possible respect, guilty, empty, false . . . well, what's to be said? And if I am wholly an innocent victim, then what's to be said? Actually, there's a lot to be said; and the saying of it is how we grow together. I was looking recently at some of Wittgenstein's notes, and he remarks in a comment from (I think) the 1940s to the effect that 'no-one can simply say, "I loathe myself" without being mad'. The only other way of saying 'I loathe myself' is to put an 'and' on the end of the sentence – '*and* it's time I did something about it. It's time I thought about it, dealt with it.'[4]

MZ Do you want to say a bit more about that?

RW The phrase which Wittgenstein uses, I think, is 'nobody can say of themselves, I am filth'. Either that's a sign of mental dissolution of some kind, or it's the stating of a feeling which has to be *thought through* and acted on; you can't just sit passively with it.

MZ In other words, it's delusional if you don't investigate the feeling through thinking and the experience of it.

RW   Scratch it a bit, turn it over in your hand. Now, what do I say about this, what do I think about this, where does this go? Self-abasement is as problematic as the completely un-selfcritical approach that claims that nothing has to be forgiven.

MZ   It is something to do with that articulation or the utterance of it, isn't it? That we can *utter*, that we can *think* about it. Thinking in a very real sense of addressing what's at hand, otherwise if you're in denial, you cannot even speak to a certain extent. I wonder where the mercy comes in or how it can be shaped, especially if you're unaware of your own complicity.

RW   That's right. Some of it comes down to the bare fact of having those you can trust somewhere to hand. We come back to the trust issue. We've had quite a lot of thinking over the past couple of decades about the erosion of trust in people and institutions, and I think that – unfortunately – this is entirely on target; because if I don't have trustworthy interlocutors and companions around, then there are some very alarming prisons to end up in.

MZ   If we come back to that idea of relation and witnessing different possibilities, I am thinking of the example of people saying 'you are welcome' to refugees, and I think it's these moments of connection that can make or break a person. I remember many years ago, at the height of the Balkan Wars, when refugees were being spread out across world, and some refugees ended up in Tasmania, of all places. They had arrived by bus and they wouldn't get off the bus. I completely understood why they wouldn't get off the bus – they had been dumped, without their choice, to the other side of the planet – but the rhetoric at the time was that these people were ungrateful and all these sorts of things like that. But they just weren't feeling safe and welcomed. Of course, then it goes the other way around where people think that it's a threat to their existence to have people enter their country and to welcome them on that very basic level.

RW Thinking about all this, it does seem that we're probably ripe for some rather deeper thinking about what we mean by families. It seems an odd connection to make ...

MZ I think it's absolutely right. It is about a different understanding of relationships ...

RW Most of us are inured to a rather short-cut discourse about 'family values', which makes many feel a bit uncomfortable, and so we ignore what the real moral importance of a family is. It's something like a sign, or witness, if you like, of all the human bonds that are not subject to renegotiation; they're just there, informing, supporting, nurturing us. Think of the very fact of childbirth, the arrival of a stranger in our midst whom we are obliged to welcome and nourish; there is something very basic about human solidarity that has to be recognised here.

MZ Isn't that the case of the Christ figure, in that way? It's always about inviting the stranger and it's about welcoming difference. And in that welcoming, you have to create bonds and you have to be present to, and to learn from, them. Which is what happens with children, but sometimes you might think, 'Oh my God, what is this?!'

RW   Yes; we don't always make a huge success of it, but we know at some level what we're meant to do with it. This may help us understand why we still recoil a bit from the possibility that childbirth and child rearing can be taken right away from the relational setting, why we sense some discomfort about too much mechanisation or 'technologisation' of the process. This discomfort is worth attending to and isn't just a bit of unenlightened prejudice.

I'm not talking about IVF and things like that, but most of us still feel that the idea, let's say, that children should routinely or normatively be conceived in test tubes and reared by state-paid crèches sounds warning bells. Part of what I think is the matter is that normally the arrival of a child – even an adopted child, for that matter – within a close relationship implies that individuals in an intimate partnership are saying, 'We trust our partnership enough to allow a new presence here. We trust our relationship to be capable of mutating into something that can nourish another.' That's the most extraordinary act of faith, but it's an act of faith that's routinely made by human beings, day after day, in every culture you can name across the world. This ought to tell us something about how we should be coping with identity and strangeness, this extraordinary fact that here, at the very centre of our thinking about human beings, is an act of faith towards the new and the strange: the trust that human intimacy, shared identity, shared commitment, when it's at its most intense, shows itself to be something oriented towards welcome.

MZ   If we extend that, then it suggests what we are working with is the bonds that we can create, and that we can have faith in and believe in. It becomes so much more problematic when the nation or the state limits welcoming or the human capacity that allows us to exist in a space of recognition.

RW To put it very simply: when we don't know who we are, we are instinctively less ready to welcome. Of course we back away from trust when we don't feel that we're secured and held, either by some individual's love or by the richness or solidity of a community, or both.

MZ It does come to this question of us thinking about respect, but I am also thinking about love in that un-graspable way where you can feel that security in relation, and if you believe in God, then that's one vehicle for it. I'm thinking of the tensions that are happening, too, with the disrespect for other faiths. It has something to do with love and its potential that can move us beyond, or embrace the extension of, the idea of family, and that enriches us in some ways.

RW There's a really interesting phrase that I have often quoted from a third-century Christian writer, where he says that the most extraordinary thing about the love of God for us is that it is love for something *with which God has nothing naturally in common*, so that the great mystery of God's love is that it is love for what is truly different. Now, that's a writer who certainly wouldn't deny that we're made in the image of God and so forth, and he isn't saying that God is innately hostile or indifferent towards us or any such thing. He is simply saying that God is infinite liberty, infinite joy, infinite intelligence, and we're not; and yet we are loved as if we *were* akin to this infinite abundance. This is love that can create the most extraordinary and unlikely kinship of all, a kinship between the finite and the infinite. For this particular writer – Clement of Alexandria – that becomes one of the things that sets in motion a chain of thinking about Christian ethics. It's not just about the people like you, not just about the people close to you.

MZ It's acceptance and faith of some sort.

RW That's right. I would guess that the Jew and the Muslim would say something similar, on the basis of a similar story of God's gratuitous creation of a world that is different from God's own divine being. We deeply misunderstand Jewish identity if we see it as selfishly exclusive rather than as a reality that declares, 'Here is a summons to a unique way of witnessing, to the possibility of community in the presence of God, a summons and response which we hope everybody else will take note of, or take heart from.' This is very close to the centre of Jewish identity, the idea that Jews are called to show that there's a law-governed, just, compassionate community that can be created by the awareness of and response to God's presence and calling. You make what you want of it, says the Jew to the rest of the world, but this is what we do.

And the Muslim sense of a fellowship, the *umma* as a people to which *anyone* can belong, makes a comparable claim. So within the Abrahamic tradition, you have all of this common vision. Within the non-Abrahamic religious traditions, you also have equivalents. It all suggests that when religious creativity, and I'd say underline the word *creativity*, is really kindled, this sense of community without barriers is one of the things that seems to come out of it. Religions, God knows, do appalling damage and get locked into different kinds of exclusivism; yet when you look at what each one of them has that's distinctive in its own context, distinctive and initially disturbing and novel, it's regularly something to do with this – the call to look again about your assumptions about sameness and difference, about insiders and outsiders. The God of Hebrew scripture reminding the people of Israel, 'You were strangers in Egypt': you were once outsiders, and you must never forget it.

MZ I had a young Muslim student who wanted to study more about the misinterpretation of Isaac and the sacrifice, and how that's often justified as violence in the Muslim tradition. She raised how you can take parts or elements of readings and rework them for your own interest, but at the core – which is what you're saying – is this fundamental question of sameness and difference. Paradoxically, most of the great 'crimes' happen because of the attachment to 'sameness', rather than the threat of difference.

RW For myself, in looking at historic religious texts, the most interesting question is always *not* how do they reflect some of the same, rather unhelpful, attitudes that their culture generally shared, especially to women or to violence, but what the things are that make them at *odds* with that consensus. You can talk until the cows come home about how this or that classical religious text inscribes patterns of patriarchy or violent exclusivism; but that's not what makes them interesting, because that's what they have in common with a lot of the ambient culture. But when you have God saying to the Israelites, 'You were outsiders, and that's why you have to treat outsiders with justice', or when, in the New Testament, you hear Paul not saying just that women should obey their husbands, but also that the husband's body belongs to his wife . . .

MZ   It turns things around.

RW   Something really new and something really generative emerges. I think we're probably at a stage in our cultural history where we need to dust off this dimension of our religious heritage.

MZ   Yes, absolutely, and now I think very much so. We need to really open up the language around it and see what we can work with.

RW   Even the most convinced secularist would have to say there are some positive things that this discourse of faith has made possible, like it or not, and we need to be clear about why that is, so that we don't just forget.

MZ   What are the elements that we can bring together to make this possible? For me, the rethinking of justice is part of this attempt to open out public language around it. How do we take those tenets of different kinds of religious sensibility and feed them back into cultural discourses? In other words, what can we learn? Because otherwise, we continue the violence. Even with what you were just saying, it isn't the violence within the text or what it says that necessarily categorises ways of thinking, it's what's outside of that. How can we become curious again? The violence is real. People are doing suicide bombings. People are dying, but how do we think through it and how do we find ways of connecting that don't keep reproducing and recreating the same forms of exclusion, which makes everything and everyone feel unsafe.

RW   Yes, one of the most powerful and risky forms of exclusion is simply to say, 'People who do these things are Not Like Us' – capital N, capital L, capital U – which would mean that we don't have to think about them. And this not thinking about them is the beginning of another turn of the great wheel of injustice and cruelty. It doesn't mean condoning, or denying, the evil of what some others do; it doesn't mean not resisting in whatever ways are possible and just, and so on. But what it does mean is the quite demanding imperative to see somebody else in the three dimensions of their actual historical and human existence.

MZ I have returned from Berlin just now, and I went to the site where the truck had driven into the Christmas market. It was a strange experience, really. What I found interesting and important was what was written on the walls in remembrance of the dead: in amongst the flowers were letters and notes saying, 'We want love, we want peace, we want all these things because we don't want to reproduce the violence.' I thought it was unique for that situation. It's not usually what we would expect or see in the media, but on the ground, people often feel strongly about violence.

RW That takes us back to the way in which people instinctively seem to show some awareness of this need to break a cycle, an instinct that we need to foreground.

MZ We need to cultivate it through modes of speech, action and thinking around tragedy and violence.

RW There is a book by a French journalist whose wife was killed in a terrorist attack; I think the title is *You Will Not Make Me Hate*,[5] and it explores how, in the face of real horror, real pain and real evil, you retain your freedom to see clearly, a freedom not to be drawn into the vortex of destructive passion.

MZ   Which is what you were saying before about *thinking* – if you say people are not like us and there is no sense of proximity or relation … The proximity or a sense of connection is what makes us human regardless of the difference, and so if you deny that connection, then you deny that thinking or feeling that relation allows you to witness and to see things. And, in a more global sense, you can watch things and not respond because there's no sense of the proximity. I think you've written about it in a different way, and it's that need for the telling of different stories, the need of the imagination here to come in and also to guide us. You need the action of that very direct witnessing level and the intuitive instinctual response to things, and you also need the creativity that can imagine how these things can happen, so stories can be told and retold.

RW   That's right. I'm not one of those who would throw around the word 'empathy' as the answer to all our problems, but the imagination to stand even very briefly in the shoes of another is a major attainment or gift. And the best of our artistic life takes us into that realm.

MZ   It gives us multiple points of view. I think it allows us not only to step into another's shoes; rather, it allows us to move across several perspectives. It's a person perceiving multiple situations … I think that's the beauty of art.

RW   Yes, and lest we get too precious about this, I believe that good soap opera for a lot of people is a real moral crucible, allowing us to see three-dimensional people reacting to extremely difficult situations and testing out how they might react in a way that the viewer or the listener can recognise as human like them. It's not as trivial as some would have it ...

MZ I think a lot of the moral and ethical testing grounds are in these realms ... where people can connect with things that might challenge them, but they might not find it in other sources.

RW You need people. And this, in turn, means that you need the right investment in education, in the training of the imagination in all these and other ways. It was very interesting talking to my colleagues in the prison discussion group the other day, and finding that these thoughts about imagination and solidarity were the ideas that made absolute sense. They were quite happy to talk about that.

MZ The training of the imagination?

RW Yes. People in a high-security prison were quite willing to say, *that's* ...

MZ That's what we need. That's what we want.

RW And the lack of it is one of the things that has got us here, in our current global mess.

MZ That's interesting. You could say that the situation that we're in globally is partly to do with the lack of training and imagination, and it's nothing to do with class or to do with accessibility in that way, and it's more to do with safety and nurturance.

RW I think so.

MZ   I'd like to round off our conversation: I think the idea of the human and the sacred is how we can imagine that relationship.

RW   To borrow something I've said elsewhere: what is often most important about our human relations is when we recognise that the other is related to something greater than me. They have an identity that's theirs, in relation to a world that I don't own and don't control; or, to put it more directly and poetically, their faces are turned toward God, as well as mine.

MZ   The mystery of which life is.

RW   That's right, and that's where they are most real, most full; and I don't have full access to that. I don't control it and I may very well say, 'I can't for the life of me see where it is or how it works for them, but I know I have to act on the assumption that it's there – the sacred, that to which all beings relate.'

MZ   I imagine that crosses sentient and non-sentient in that sense.

RW   I think it does.

MZ   We're foregrounding the human in this instance, but the non-human is as important in recognising this relationship.

RW   One of the most moving experiences I've had in months was visiting an exhibition in South Africa of cave painting, 'Bushman', art from the San people of South Africa. I watched a film there about a hunt and a dance in one of these tribal groups. As with so many premodern people, the hunt is an intensely ritualised, mythological and spiritual experience. You're not just slaughtering an animal, but you acknowledge that the animal is sacred; and by some extraordinary dispensation, the divine gives you this animal not just for food, but also in some way as 'spirit'.

In the San culture, when you slaughter an eland you release its spirit into yourself; they have a very visible reverence for the dying animal and this is something that marks the hunt and the killing as a deeply sacred moment. It is all about the animal's relation to the depth, the interior world, which, when you kill and eat it, you are incorporated into in some way. It's a very intense transaction when you see it on film; and, of course, it's what you see in all the cave paintings in South Africa – the different aspects and moments in the hunt. It's significant, too, that many San folktales begin with the formula, 'When people were animals and animals were people ...'

MZ   Yes, so that you are equal in a sense.

RW   And there is a wonderful proverb from the San, which was quoted in one of these films, 'We do not know where God lives, but the eland does.'

PART THREE

LOVE

In this last part, Rowan and I reflect and build upon the different approaches and considerations of how to justly attend to others and ourselves, and we discuss the important relationship between justice and love. We explore how to cultivate responses of love and patience in a wider political sense, and we investigate how religion and certain ideas of faith have given us tools to address these relations of love, suffering and justice, and how to live in a just world. These tools, we suggest, do not bind us to religions, but may attract us to the spiritual dimensions of our lives and the very practical considerations of care and attention that are necessary to the creation of thoughtful communities.

Through a kind of phenomenology of understanding, we consider how to *think about thinking*, where thought provides us with the imaginative capacity to understand some of the common fates that we share – in global and local terms – in response to climate change, the refugee experience, and the aftermath of war and other atrocities. We seek to engage with the thinking that might lead us toward meaningful dialogue and exchange in our individual and public lives. Creating the imaginative space in which we can find ways to invent, listen and respond to humanitarian, environmental or political crisis is a challenge but essential to the cartography and beauty of justice.

Finally, we consider the need to renew our social bonds within a framework of gratitude, which recognises their relational, rather than contractual, quality. In so doing, we examine love and justice as inseparable from the task of responding ethically to each other and to the world.

VI

For Love and Justice

October 2017

MZ We've previously spoken about how to expand on the language of justice and how to find an alternative language for it. Over the course of our conversations, there's been some interesting issues that have emerged around the idea of global witnessing and questions of suffering. To my mind, this involves the need to *think about thinking*, which is something that you have written about. And if we take seriously the need to respond to the complexity of suffering and different approaches to it, then there is a necessary relationship between love and justice.

I'd say that even the most committed secularist would recognise that religion – and certain ideas of faith – have given us tools to address these relations of love, suffering, justice and so on. And I'm interested in how to engage with these elements in a public environment, and how to invite an understanding or bridge across secularist and religious themes in public discourse, so as to help create a healthy and open environment, and to learn ways to take moral responsibility toward the world. But I'd like to start with something to do with the idea of global witnessing and the relationship of love and justice to it.

RW   The question of love and justice is something which I find myself coming back to often. Have you seen Regina Schwartz's recent book on Shakespeare, *Loving Justice, Living Shakespeare*?[1]

It's basically a book on love and justice in Shakespeare's drama, looking at the connection between love and *accurate vision*: it works on the assumption that to give somebody the attention that they deserve is love *and* it is also justice. The two are inseparable. So to spend the time needed – and *time* is a key idea here – to get to know, to see, to hear somebody is to treat them justly. It's also crucial to how we think about love. So the lack of love and the lack of justice belong together: and this shows up in habits of haste, dismissiveness, the refusal to see, the refusal to hear, the refusal to take time. And if you're in a very pressured cultural environment where time doesn't get taken very much, it's not surprising if both love and justice go out of the window.

MZ   Yes, and throughout our conversations we've been talking about or referring in one way or another to the idea of patience, attention and the consequences of not having time. There's something about time, patience and attention that is central to justice. We have been discussing some of this in relation to Iris Murdoch's work,[2] and some of the issues of morality and action and the good. Now I want to think more about it in the context of where we are at the moment, and looking at big-picture issues such as violence: how do we cultivate responses of time and attention, and how do love and justice fit together in all of this? How do we *see* accurately as a form of justice in the wider political sense?

RW At the moment, we're in a political environment or public culture where polarisation is, if you want to put it this way, the 'sexy' thing, the exciting thing: people get their energy from extreme polarisation, and this naturally fosters an *unjust* attitude. It creates a situation where – as in the UK or the US – you end up with a political process that leaves 50 per cent of the population feeling not only that they have lost, but that they have been disenfranchised. It's not just that a certain phase in ongoing public discussion has happened, has been decided, but that people are being made to feel that if you lost, even by a small margin, your opinion doesn't count, your perspective doesn't count.

I'm thinking of the way in which, in this country, a language of 'the will of the people' and 'enemies of the people' is suddenly being revived for the 48 per cent of the population who didn't vote the desired way in the Brexit referendum; and this really does disturb me.

MZ If I understand what you're saying, then, it's the production of this kind of opposition that hinders the possibility or the enactment of love and justice.

RW Yes. And I think, therefore, it is affecting adversely the idea that you can have a just democracy, because if all you've got is a succession of majorities, then how do you attend to the people who are left? To the people in the minority?

MZ So how do we create the environment that acknowledges this sense of the 'unjust'? What modes of intervention are possible? There's something very important about *thinking about suffering* and *thinking about thinking*, and how these are linked together. In other words, it seems to be about trying to get the complexity of this experience and how to make sense of the reality that we are engaged in every day.

RW   I think this is where educational and community institutions need to practise debate and discussion at the local level far more intentionally and innovatively. I was talking to somebody just a couple of days ago about a raft of new educational initiatives in this country, looking at how you conduct disagreement, how you handle irreconcilable news, how you recognise that the other person is not going away, and that, therefore, a final line cannot be drawn.

At the moment, I'm investigating, with a number of people in the UK, the question of how we can better resource this kind of educational practise across the board. I suspect also that we haven't got enough contexts in this country where real public debate, real public discernment goes on. It's a point that's often been made about how we conduct our election campaigns these days. We have rallies, we have high-profile statements, we have mass communication and all the drama of celebrity politics. We have rather less of the town hall meeting. But, to come back to a familiar point, how do we recover that dimension of a political life?

MZ   This has something to do with time: the process of time and the unfolding of time, and that when you're in an environment that feels conflictual or reactive or oppositional, say, in the public sense, then to insert time or a certain kind of patience in response to other people or differences is what we've lost – and what we've lost in our daily lives. So, how do we practically take on board what you're suggesting: that is, responding in an educational setting or in a community environment to reactivity? What enables us to take into serious consideration that working in opposition shuts down discussion and debate, and to recognise that debate doesn't have to be about opposite sides – it can be about working out the intricacies of an issue or a disagreement?

RW   I think there are two points there: one is that if I'm right, I need to learn more of what it *means* to be right – in terms of what I now know I must do, what I now know of how I must speak or relate. Even if I am 'right', my learning continues, and so does my capacity to listen. So the second thing, of course, is that no one has to be right to be worth listening to.

I don't have to silence opposition in order to guarantee my worth, my right to be there, my right to be a part of this. That's why I think a lot of this has to do with a deep insecurity about whether *I have the right to be heard*. People talk about the Trump phenomenon or the Brexit phenomenon very much in terms of people who feel disenfranchised, who feel their voices are habitually not heard. Naturally, therefore, there's a resonance with people who say to them, 'I'll show you how to be triumphant and secure, how to be right. I'll show you how to win.' *And then you'll know ... Then you'll be safe.* Then there will be no doubt at all about your access to the public debate.

But what if you belong to a community where your position is assured, your dignity is guaranteed, and you don't have to be winning all the time to be part of it? A community where you don't constantly have to earn your place? I think one of the things that we're in danger of losing in our polarised political atmosphere is this vision of a community where we belong without the obligation to earn our position. And, of course, the church and other religious groups are – or should be – there to remind society of the possibility of such a level of belonging.

MZ   The implication of what you're saying, if I'm understanding it correctly, is that the point about *not being right* and the point *about being right* is that you have to learn in both cases. So how do you learn to listen? It's a different framework. It's a framework that's not about a dialectic, but of recognising your participation in the act of creating a community.

RW   There is meaning—

MZ   Yes, and how to create meaning out of what doesn't exist, meaning out of non-meaning, in some ways, and particularly when it's the silencing of debate and when terror or violence happens. How do we shake up all of those things?

RW   If we can assume that our humanity is about learning, then learning takes time; therefore, a just society is, among other things, one that enables everybody to do the learning they need to do and take the time they need to take.

MZ   How can we progress that? Obviously, art allows a certain kind of movement in that direction, and we've talked about different creative works that allow us those ways to see and to hear, and also to train the imagination. I wonder about those dimensions. How do they become part of this question of right and of having to learn, even if you are right?

RW   It relates to some of the work I've sometimes been involved in around education, about what the good school or university might look like. The most inspiring university course I've been involved in is in the 'Modern Liberal Arts' course at Winchester, where I've had the joy of being an external examiner in recent years. It's really a general cultural/political programme where the focus is all the time on the nature of learning. They do a lot of work with primary texts, and they do a lot of work on the nature of the authority of the teacher, and the nature of freedom as you discover it in the process of learning.

Every year I come away from my examining thinking, 'Why isn't everybody doing this course?' And I think there's a bit more attention in some higher-education circles on this sort of issue. I saw a book recently by Alan Jacobs, who's at Baylor University in the United States, basically on how to argue, how to develop a culture of reasoned argument.[3] It's rather depressing that you need books to tell you how to do it, but we do at the moment.

The tension is that at the very moment where we desperately need this, a lot of the ethos of higher-education institutions, as well as other educational institutions, seems to be pushing in an opposite direction, pushing towards a very functional, problem-solving mode of work. We need 'impact' and 'output' and lots of measurable effect, and so we end up where we started this conversation: the problem that we don't think much about thinking.

MZ   That does seem to be the case in the Western context, at least. And as a consequence, there's a generation of younger people who are teaching, who are losing sight, for want of a better word, of the real questions that are at stake with learning. The impact of this change in

ethos affects how we define what is valuable or not valuable in our
cultures.

That's where that relationship of love comes in, and in a previous
conversation you mentioned how God's love – and you quoted a
third-century Christian writer – is always about loving the
'uncommon'.[4] So, in other words, love involves imperfection, yet we
tend to live our lives on the basis that we always have to be right. I find
that there's something very interesting about this idea of imperfection
and the 'uncommon'. Do you have anything more you want to say
about this relationship?

RW   I think that the point about the third-century Christian writer
I mentioned, Clement of Alexandria, was in what he says about God's
love – that God doesn't simply love what's like God; God just loves
what's there, He doesn't go around looking for things that remind
Him of God. He just loves what's there, what He's made, which is not
Him. And that's the basis for imagining a kind of love which just loves
what's *there* and doesn't look for the things that are simply feedback –
what's OK and what makes me feel OK – but engages me with what is
actually in front of me.

I think that's an important dimension of what faith brings in here;
but, of course, the irony is that while I think you and I would probably
agree that religious faith when it's doing its job is working like this, at
the same time it's so often one of the major things that intensifies
people's anxieties about being right, and so intensifies their failures in
love and justice.

MZ   Which is a strange paradox, isn't it? Coming back to that
question of love and justice, if there is some understanding of loving

what is there, then that means – in terms of difference or in rightness – you have to engage with all that you encounter. The word that's coming to mind is 'wretchedness', and the possibility of living with your own and another's wretchedness or imperfection.

RW Yes, and therefore what we aim for isn't perfection; it's the ability to put one foot in front of the other gracefully, knowing that this is not 'it', but nonetheless I can act, I can relate, and I can learn. The great thing about talking about learning is that it's a language of hope; it's something that will enrich, that will enlarge, and it's out there. And if we can only somehow convey the idea that to say I have more to learn is not an admission of weakness, but an expression of hope or even hunger, this surely is one of the major educational messages that we should strive to try and communicate.

MZ This seems to be connected with wisdom, but a different kind of wisdom. It's not exactly the same as the wisdom Plato speaks about in the *Symposium*, where Socrates is in search of, or unveils, the true meaning of wisdom. It seems a much more grounded wisdom, or it's a wisdom that comes out of action in the practical world, or engagement with the world.

RW I think so. And that's where you need Aristotle as well as Plato; you need *phronesis*, practical sense. You need literally the common *sense*, the capacity to run your hand down the grain of the things, the texture of things, and work your way, feel your way. We've probably talked before about the importance of a modern philosopher like Merleau-Ponty and his emphasis on the body and learning. We learn to know things *because we are bodies*, not because we are disembodied minds.

Our minds make maps and charts for us to navigate a world of unexpected resistance and solidity and complexity. We learn how to sit on chairs, and how to stand up, and how to walk across the room. You watch a nine-month-old baby learning, and it's learning to *think,* not just learning how to avoid bumping its head; it's learning to think, to map the world. This excites me, the thought that our knowledge, our deepest intellectual capacities, originate at that level of not bumping into things. That's when we start forming concepts.

MZ There are two things related to this: one is Merleau-Ponty's own kind of spiritual sense and how that might interconnect with his mappings of the world and navigations, and the related point, for me, is where does faith in the world and the growing sense of interrelatedness take shape? In other words, if *it is* our bodies that learn to navigate space, how does that corporeality and groundedness shape the capacity to love or the capacity to feel?

RW I think it's extraordinary that when we encounter those bits of matter that are other people's bodies, we learn to read them. It seems we instantly recognise what a smile says. You see it with babies and young children. It happens very early, and there's an immediate bond. When you think about it, that's quite strange: here is this other bit of stuff in the world, it behaves in a certain way, it looks like this rather than like that, and you *read* it, you don't just register it. You say 'friendly/unfriendly'. You say 'nourishing/not nourishing'. And it's the same as learning to look into somebody else's eyes and gauge their feeling or their response. You learn to decode.

One of the things that interests me most in some neuroscientific research these days is the examination of what happens when certain bits of the brain stop functioning, when people's capacity to read another person's face is lost or impaired, as happens sometimes – the sort of distortion that doesn't allow them to pick up meanings. It's as if our entire psychophysical system – our thinking, our feeling, our sensing – is all kind of bundled up together in this process of learning to navigate, learning to read, and, on the basis of that, making the maps and the charts that show us where to go.

MZ I'm thinking about the difficulties for people when they're deprived, and who may not have the same freedoms to navigate the world, and that Merleau-Ponty is very important to all of this and how to navigate difficulties in the world.

RW To me, the most important thing Merleau-Ponty reminds us of is that the world of sensoria that we're always experiencing is not self-explanatory or self-organised. We make the connections ... as I say, we read the signals, but we read them as physical beings, we don't read them in the abstract, as minds in isolation.

When I first read Merleau-Ponty, one passage that made a clear and lasting impression was where he discusses putting your hand on the desk where you're sitting, and feeling both the top side and the underside. He says in effect: now, how does your mind put together an *object* from these sense impressions? That's what the mind does, it constructs an object because it assumes dimensionality, diverse and convergent points of orientation, and so on. That's how we work, how we 'navigate' the world we share.

MZ Yes, and in relation to the ideas of faith and love and justice, and our experiences which are corporeal in that way and environmental, how do you think they fit together – the navigating of these kind of sensorial and embodied realities in relation to others and ourselves? It seems crucial.

RW   It seems to me that if our knowing is always negotiating, feeling our way and making those maps or charts that I talked of, then there's something about the essence of our human being and well-being which is bound up with knowing how to navigate successfully, at a number of very different levels – from how not to fall over something in the middle of the room when you're nine months old, to how not to ignore or derealise or dehumanise the other person with whom you're in connection.

So in this context, love and justice are not just extra things put in to make us nicer than what we might otherwise be. They are deeply bound up with our lives, our well-being. The person who habitually, compulsively ignores or demeans the reality of another is the person who is, at the end of the day, sacrificing their own well-being. Whatever they may think, they are eroding their very life.

MZ   There's something that's very, very deep and, in a way, almost at a level unknown, because you can't consciously think of everything at the same time: there are many dimensions of reality and experience. And perhaps that's part of the mystery, or that's what makes us attuned to people – the fact that either we accept the navigation of our corporeality of our lives, our engagements, or we refuse them, right?

RW   That's right. And the way I've sometimes put this is that it's a sense of not *owning* the other person, knowing that they relate to something more than me. And when I react to someone else with respect or with attention, it's partly in this conviction that their relationship with myself is only a small part of what they are, and that they're related to a literally immeasurably broad background of relatedness – people, things, realities, dimensions, which make them who they are.

And ultimately, as a religious person, I'd say they are related to God. I connect that with the way Saint Paul speaks in the letter to the Romans about not judging your Christian neighbour for what they do because they're not *yours*. They don't belong to you. They are serving somebody else (Romans 14). And that's a kind of ethical point of orientation, I believe – the fact that they are related to somebody else, and that they're not answerable to you for what they do.

MZ If that's the case, and if we come back to ideas of right that we were talking about earlier, even if you are right, you have to learn from it; and if you're not, you've still got to learn from it. You can't own the discourse or the language of another. That's where acceptance comes in. I think the language of acceptance can be useful, but it involves something else as well . . .

RW It can't be just shrugging your shoulders and saying, 'Well, I can't do anything about that.' It's a bit more active and interactive. And that something more is, I suppose, 'All right, so I don't own the other person; so what is it they know that I don't, or that they see and I don't? And exactly how am I going to find that out and work with it?' The answer surely is by talking with them.

That's the thing about language, isn't it? On the one hand, it's taking the great risk of speaking and not quite knowing what resistance or incomprehension there may be; on the other hand, it's not knowing what might come back that will enrich and enlarge. What I don't know and don't see is perhaps one aspect of what I need to 'navigate' better as I encounter it.

MZ What you were saying before about Merleau-Ponty and navigation, it is exactly that: it's the navigating of the mind in a more nimble sense, with its conceptual contours, which is about a deep sense of connection, and that we don't always understand what it means to be in those moments; but by taking risks, we are given the potential to learn other ways of communicating because we're opening ourselves up to chance, to difference . . .

RW That's why the bare fact of language is so important. As I said, we learn to read noises, gestures, eye contact – and all of that is language, something we read as meaningful and respond to meaningfully. We respond, we take the risk of entering this game. And that's where learning happens.

The whole 'navigating' aspect of our growing and learning is, as one philosophical tradition would say, 'analogical'. You begin by simply finding your way around physically; and then you find your way around with increasing skill in the characteristically human interactions of language and culture. And if you're a religious person, you might ultimately find your way around in relation to that all-encompassing agency and mystery out of which love comes.

MZ I'm interested in that mystery, in the religious sense, as it can be part of our orientation. And even if you're not religious, there's still something in the engagement that propels love and the possibility for it, whether you believe or not.

RW   That's right.

MZ   Thinking about all of this makes me return to the question of justice and the question of beauty. I'm thinking about the article by Elaine Scarry on 'Beauty and the Scholar's Duty to Justice',[5] where she talks about how there's the need to bring to students the complexity of beauty in relation to ethical responsibilities and understanding the world, and that beauty is not an esoteric thing; it's something practical. And by kind of engaging in this, people can learn the possibility of love or learn the possibilities of justice and freedom. Just as you were saying earlier about the course at Winchester, it's something about those dimensions that can open out our hearts and minds.

RW   Yes, and talking about beauty is a difficult area because, again, we've tended to lose the robust medieval sense that the good, the true and the beautiful belong together. When we say it now, it sounds a bit woolly, perhaps just aesthetic, all about nice things that make us feel better. And that's not it.

I think the medieval language gives us a strong and coherent picture to think through; there are moments where we see order and connectedness in such intensity that it feels like a revelation of the real. When people in the Thomist tradition talk about beauty as *splendour formae*, the radiance of form, this points to the way that 'formal' connection operates not just as a series of solved problems, but as giving some utterly unexpected insight into the depth of things, into the fact that this is how the world is: a system of connection, interweaving, exchange of life, a system literally of radiant energy. Beauty of very different kinds does that. It may be simply the beauty of a physical prospect, a physical landscape where you sense the interweaving of light and contour and material (for me, that is the sun that goes down on the sea off the West Wales coast). And you think, 'Yes, that's it.'

Or it may be, more paradoxically, something like the end of *King Lear*, a representation of human extremity that is terrible, and yet you recognise that something has 'come together'; Yeats's 'terrible beauty', perhaps, and Rilke's beauty as the beginning of terror.[6] And there's the beauty of a battered or ageing human face that expresses experience, history, love given and received, even when what you see is not conventionally lovely or harmonious. It's hard to talk about beauty partly because of the risk of sentimentality; you don't want to invoke a sort of greeting-card emotionalism. But to recognise these moments as moments for one to sense the real, the completely other, the completely demanding, and the completely inviting, all there in front of you, that is what matters in thinking of beauty.

MZ   It does come back to that idea of the sense of attention, which allows for the opening out of beauty, and this relatedness is about that recognition or living with the imperfections of life that is the element for learning and justice. For me, the love of the imperfect relates to a form of global witnessing that we spoke about previously: witnessing another person is a witnessing of their potential, and their beauty, which is not at all a sentimental state, but it is a more robust worldliness that enhances you because you are in contact with an experience that is not yours.

Nothing is being take from you. It's not a debt economy. This exchange involves gratitude, in a sense. It's about another economy of value and of life and of justice that has evaporated. And I'm not lamenting it, in that sense, and there's nothing nostalgic about it. There's something very practical and very real about the need for this relatedness. If we go back to the concept of navigation, it's about navigating a world and navigating our place in relation to it.

RW Yes. In that sense, beauty is also to do with an awareness of ... I suppose the best word might be 'abundance': that is, what I am encountering or what is encountering me is an *overflow* of being, reality as 'excessive' and also as inviting, not closed or exhausted. It declares that what I can see, hear, understand or cope with at any one moment isn't the whole thing. Back to the question of learning – there's more to enrich, more to discover.

And one of the things that goes wrong with the human mind or psyche is when it locks itself into a model of scarcity and reduction. 'There's not enough to go around' is the root of a lot of problems.

MZ Yes, and it creates more problems because you're not willing to, in effect, *give* in any particular way; whether it's resources or whether it's charity, in that sense, the charity that we've been talking about, which is about some sense of alignment or some sense of recognition of others and their destitution. This is a different path and way to understand justice, which is about understanding that is very corporeal, very sensorial, very everyday and something very human – and non-human as well.

RW This question of what you might call the 'dignity', or the 'worth', of the everyday, the significance of the prosaic, and the need to take time observing is central. I've just been reading, quite coincidentally, a wonderful short story by a Dutch writer, which describes a writer going out with a radio journalist to a remote rural part of Holland to interview a local rat catcher.[7]

The journalist is absolutely determined to make this a complex and rather symbolic episode about conflicts between urban and rural life and tensions around life and death. But both the writer and the rat catcher only want to talk about rats, how to catch them and why you have to catch them. Long discussions unfold about the habits of muskrats in the dykes of the Netherlands, the risks they run, the way in which their coats change at different seasons, why buzzards like to eat dead muskrats – detail upon detail upon detail.

And at every point where the conversation takes off into that kind of rich detail, the journalist switches off his tape recorder because he says that this is boring: he wants ideas. I think the whole point of this really wonderful little story is that ideas don't matter as much as *attention* – or, at least, that ideas are worthless unless they're able to cope with the habits of muskrats.

MZ   Yes, that's right! I really love this image, because it's, in fact, the *detail* of the everyday that allows you to respond to situations – the real detail of life and experience. I'm thinking of immediate situations, where something might unfold in front of you – whether it be a crisis, or whether it be somebody suffering or somebody dying, or whatever it might be – and you're compelled to respond because you're attentive, and you're looking at the detail, and you're reading it, but reading it in a much more profound way. It's that connectedness of the spirit in navigating life, and the deeper sense of it.

RW What we're after, educationally speaking, is training in the habits of attention, the habits of seeing the everyday. And it's harder than it sounds.

MZ Yes. It is absolutely about this training in the habits of attention. I was having a discussion with a taxi driver the other day, and it was just after the Las Vegas shooting that occurred at the Harvest Music festival.[8] And I hadn't heard about it because I had been travelling, and I had just arrived home.

This driver was saying that he had done some investigations into gun shootings in America, and he did some figures – I can't remember exactly what there were, but it was something like 439,000 people in America each year are murdered by each other, or suicides, or other fatal shootings. It made me think that fear is always the fear from the outside, but it is actually our own non-attention to others, to our own experiences that can often create the violence. In some ways, the terror exists within our own lives. And what we call 'terror', or the discourses it generates, is always directed to others, other people, other cultures; but we haven't addressed some of our own propensities toward violence.

RW That's as much as to say that attention has to be turned onto ourselves as well as others. We need to attend to ourselves with the same kind of patience and, in the proper sense, detachment with which we attend to others. The word 'detachment' is a bit of a challenge, I know: we haven't got a word, unfortunately, that doesn't sound a bit chilly. 'Dispassionate' won't quite do either. But it's meant to evoke the careful, judicious, unjudging looking which says, 'Mmm, so that's what I'm like', just as you might look at another person and say, 'Mmm, so that's what they're like' – not immediately starting with how this is going to make me feel better or worse, but just taking the time to look at oneself with patience and clarity. That's every bit as hard as looking at others, possibly harder, but it's all related.

MZ   Yes, learning new habits.

RW   It's one of the things that certain kinds of Buddhist teachers will underline – that you need to learn to look at yourself with the same kind of dispassionate eye as you look at another. You observe what's happening and say, 'So that's happening. This is "arising"' – a key Buddhist idiom. 'This is "arising"': 'I see in myself that this kind of reaction happens. Well and good. Now, let's look at it carefully.'

MZ   And it is the hardest thing to translate into the public discourse and language, which I think is something, too, about what you're saying about *right* – having to learn even if you are right, and then having to learn if you're not right. It's about that ability to attend to this reality in negotiations. And we just don't do it in diplomacy or in a detailed responsibility towards how we measure or gather information.

RW   I went to a workshop a few weeks ago at a conference I attended on listening, a workshop conducted by a professional hostage negotiator. He said, 'I want to talk to you about listening when it really is *literally* a matter of life and death'; and he was telling us about the tactics he employed when he had to listen to what a hostage-taker was saying.

MZ   What were the insights that you gained from the workshop? There's something very important in this attention to listening.

RW There was a great deal about how you clear your mind of your private agenda, and also about some of the things you need to do in your body so as to attend better. I won't attempt a full summary of it, but it was that kind of thing.

MZ How do you respond to situations in which a violent act is unfolding? How do you learn to listen? People can make these things sound trite, in a way, but, in fact, it's a much deeper sense of well-being, of a potential well-being, and love.

RW And because of that, you have permission, you have licence to take time to be silent, not to try to get on top of the situation straight away, not to have to be *right* straight away. To be the sort of person who, in a crisis, instantly runs around issuing orders in order to seem decisive is not necessarily the best reaction. You need someone who will look, rub their hand along the grain of the situation – to use that image again – and get some sense of what will fit, what will work, what will go with the grain in that unique situation. Loving attention; just patience.

VII

Discourses of Faith

February 2019

MZ As we're coming to the end of these conversations, I want to talk to you about the discourses of faith. We've discussed how we have inherited different religious themes and virtues, and there is a sense that they can be helpful in navigating the world and themes of justice, but we don't really acknowledge them in a public sense. How can they be useful, or what different ways can we approach 'faith' in that sense, the connection between people, without necessarily evoking religious discourse?

RW In my mind, there are three different levels at which that can work. First, we might think of the faith that sense can be made, that we are capable of connecting with each other, *making* sense of and with each other and of our environment; the faith that we are actually capable of constructing a shared world, and of being committed to that, as something which is not just a construct but connects us with one another and with reality.

All that is an act of faith, one that has its roots historically (just as a matter of fact) in the sense that we are in some way *participating in an*

intelligible order, that the consistency of our environment is something
we can depend on. I know it's not exactly guaranteed or capable of
being mapped precisely, but it exhibits consistent patterns – which is
why, of course, we can't depend on things just carrying on according
to our convenience; there are things that we're not in control of and
will just happen whether we like it or not, like environmental
degradation. Whether or not people sign up to the root vision from
which this evolves, it is nonetheless a carry-over in some ways from
that vision.

A second area where 'faith' is at work is that it's very hard to imagine
turning the clock back on a recognition of universal and equal
approaches to human dignity – certainly in the Western world, but
also more widely – because, for good and bad reasons, 'Western'
values have a global currency these days. The notion that different
kinds of human being have radically different worth or dignity, that
deserve radically different levels of respect, is just not something that
we could easily bring back into our discourse now – which is all to the
good. So anybody now mounting a defence of slavery, let's say, or even
of torture, will have their work cut out.

And this involves another act of faith, an act of faith in humanity.
Again, it's a carry-over from a variety of religious and metaphysical
perspectives in which something is affirmed simply about being
human; there is an assumption that common humanity makes
possible a level of understanding and of . . . well, I hesitate to use the
word empathy here because it's a bit of a short-cut, but something to
do with recognising each other as feeling, desiring, suffering beings.

Yet this is a perspective that is not uncontroversial. It's not so
obvious that we can lazily take it for granted in a world where some

very toxic practises persist or are slipping back in. Forms of slavery still exist. Forms of torture still exist. To be clear that these are insupportable entail an act of faith, rooted ultimately in a variety of religious, mythological, philosophical assumptions which don't always come to the surface.

And then the third area, in some ways the hardest to bring into focus, is the practical confidence we show day by day in the meaningfulness of our free actions. We can't actually behave as if we were automata. The paradox (and there are numerous paradoxes here) is that if I were convinced by a determinist view of the world, I would still have a choice about whether I behaved like a determinist (whatever that would look like). Endless regressions there, I think.

MZ   This point about meaningful action is interesting. In terms of the discourses of faith and relationships to justice, the parameters of meaningful action seem very loaded, but also seem incredibly practical.

RW   It's very practical; and this is where it connects with justice, the question of what is the *appropriate* response to a human being, and how we clarify that in meaningfully regular ways. It isn't difficult to see the outlines of how we distinguish between 'appropriate' and 'inappropriate' responses to a human being. If we see, let's say, a car driving straight towards a pedestrian on an open road, we might very well say there's something wrong with the driver's responses to a human being. If we see somebody watching with indifference as a small child runs towards a cliff edge, we say there's something amiss. There is a response that seems to us 'proper', that makes sense, and there are responses that we would have to say don't make sense. And the notion of justice, you might say, has its roots in that kind of perception, that kind of awareness of which responses 'make sense'.

MZ   That's interesting, too – the idea of sensibility and the idea of being sensitive to another. There is a connection between meaningful acts and being sensitive, and so often, we're not sensitive to, or rather, we may consider what's appropriate or inappropriate, but we don't actually sense those bits in-between, which are not always clear.

RW   It's certainly worth noting that our cultural development in the last few decades has put down more and more markers about the things we ought to be aware of in respect of how we're heard, how we're experienced by less privileged others. And while people may sneer at 'trigger warnings' and the 'snowflake generation' and all the rest of it, we have actually grown a little bit in our awareness. We've learned something about how appropriate response to somebody else means a level of imaginative recognition, an understanding of why they may respond in this particular way, and we can no longer just override this learning in how we now behave.

MZ   I'm not convinced that's the case ... I don't think we have enough of that imaginative training.

RW   Fair enough, I suspect we don't. But what I'm really drawing attention to is that this is on the radar in a new way; so that when people start worrying about giving offence, or when people start putting into print warnings such as, 'This article contains material about x, y, and z', we are reminded of things that we have now come to recognise *as a culture*. I noticed lately in one of the student papers an article on an aspect of gender relations in the university, and at the beginning, there was an italicised subheading saying, 'This article contains reference to sexual abuse.' I don't know that we're any more literate about it all in much of our institutional as well as individual lives, but people are now flagging it, and saying, that this is an area where we've somehow got to continue to grow and change. And it can't be reversed.

MZ This relates somehow to the realm of meaningful action?

RW I think so, yes. Quite clearly, if what I say and what I do carries on regardless of the effect on another's perception of where they are in the world, I have to ask, is this a meaningful interaction with somebody else? No. To some extent, it de-solidifies, de-realises the other person, as if I'm saying to myself, 'Well, how you feel about this is none of my business.' In other words, it's an area where we're not going to communicate, there's no shared world, which is a bit of a counsel of despair.

MZ The act of faith, or what we might be calling the discourses of faith, is about the potential to recognise that?

RW Yes. The word 'recognition' is one that I keep coming back to again and again in this respect.

MZ I think it's a good one. But you were also earlier talking about the intelligible order, and how there's some faith in the fact that there is a world in which we live and inhabit, and how this aspect of 'universal' order provides a coherent sense of connection.

RW Quite simply put, the extraordinary thing is that we can talk in continuous, coherent ways about the world around us. I recall David

Hume's wonderful remark about people who claimed that they could function without assuming something about cause and effect – you may theorise about this, but when you leave the room, I shall see whether you go out by the door or by the window.

And, again, the extraordinary thing in our current culture is that while we constantly talk up the scientific world view, at the same time our timescales for cause and effect seem to be shrinking so that we can't see beyond the immediate, in terms of time. With environmental issues, we have all the evidence of how cause and effect works in the environment, and yet we say, 'Oh, it can't be that bad', or 'Somebody will sort it out', or 'We'll think of something.' As if we really weren't thinking in terms of the abiding coherence of the world around us.

MZ There's a real need and necessity in understanding how to enable that 'order', but it seems there's a blockage – when you have all the evidence and yet you still can't respond.

RW I think the fundamental thing behind some of these blockages is that I can't believe that my will is really going to be frustrated; I cannot believe that the universe could be so insensitive as not to deliver what I want.

MZ It's not narcissism, because it's too big a misunderstanding for that. The effects don't even fit the word; it's something to do with the idea of seeing and attention that we've talked about. It's those things, but it's also something else. I want to talk about the idea of abundance, which is slightly different to this point, but there is a sense of abundance that doesn't assume that I can continually get what I want. In other words, it's not that the environment is endlessly at our disposal, but it is the idea of abundance in itself which might offer a different approach to the continual degradation of the world?

RW   That's a large question. But I think there are two basic myths about humanity that help us understand the collisions here. The first involves the difference between a sense of where I am in the world that recognises fully how I am constantly being shaped and being fed by the world I'm in – that I am what I am because there is water and air and food, animals and other human subjects and all the rest of it.

The opposite, the rival picture, is one that sees me as an individual out there foraging against a hostile environment from which I've got to squeeze and grab what's necessary. The former assumes abundance not in the sense that there's infinite stuff for me to exploit, but in the sense that the world is such that I am naturally and regularly a *recipient of life*. The other model, which says we're all competing for very scarce material, assumes that we are innately positioned over and against others and the environment.

MZ   The former is more about, kind of, gratitude, isn't it?

RW   Gratitude is basic, I would say.

MZ   Gratitude is interesting, because if you start from a point of gratitude, it's a more robust attitude to life.

RW   I think so.

MZ   But how do you cultivate it? It's almost like the discourses of faith.

RW   It's an interesting mixture, because gratitude in relation to the environment is both a sense of wonder and astonishment that the world should be like this, that I should be receiving what's flowing to me, and also a kind of *settled* sense: yes, this is how it is. I can, as it were, gratefully expect it to be the way it is, because the world is *dependable* in significant ways. I don't mean by that to peddle a kind of Pollyanna-ish picture of everything everyone needs just being to hand for everyone all the time. There are real issues of the appropriate distribution of resources – issues of *justice* – but you still have to think, What's the basic story you're telling? Is it a narrative of abundance and interlocking agency? Gratitude depends on a twofold sense of wonder: surprise that the world should be like this and a sort of contemplative gratitude that the sun rises regularly each day – there is a reality that 'keeps coming', keeps offering to you.

MZ   That links to love and that kind of mystery element . . .

RW   Exactly. If you live in a world where something keeps 'coming', then the model you have of the reality in which you are living is one in which something is taking an initiative towards you. Or, at least, that's a natural implication of how you see the world. There is a pattern, a shape, to the world's life, in which my life and my well-being are a natural element in the whole picture; and, to turn that into the highly personal language of religion, this is saying that around us there is *giving not just gift*, in the environment. And maybe that is one of the most fundamental aspects of the religious sense, the sense that there is 'giving'.

MZ   I think that distinction of *giving*, rather than the gift, is important. It enables that sense abundance as a different category of experience, and the potential of connection to others.

RW Yes. It's not just the gift, not just the stuff that comes, but the fact that the sheer consistency and immeasurable interwoven complexity of all these systems is working towards where I am, where we are. It seems to me that it's a very strange use of our intellect to say that the intellectual life of human beings has evolved over the millennia in order that the intellect may dismantle the sense of gift or wonder.

MZ Yes, yes ... It's shooting yourself in the foot, so to speak—

RW Or sawing off the branch you're sitting on. I still find that a very odd thing about mechanistic pictures of the universe.

MZ There's something we were touching on about the mind itself being abundant, how it's about giving and receiving, the openness that you need as a self or being in the world.

RW Yes. The mind is not just a problem-solving mechanism. This is something I keep coming back to in my thinking: that mind is repeatedly generating new questions for itself, new imaginative projections which reshape the very problem they're trying to solve. And I've suggested here and there in the past that this is one of the differences between an organism and a machine. Machines are designed to solve problems that are fed into them; organisms both create and then 'manage' their own problems. They adjust, they evolve. And while people will say, 'Yes, but machines increasingly do that, they "learn" new behaviours', the fact remains that machines are solutions to problems that are *presented* to them in the first instance from outside their own workings. I still think there's something to be said for that as a distinction, though I have had arguments with philosophers about this.

MZ Yes, there is a whole other language around how machines themselves think, so there's that issue. What's interesting is the beauty of the mind that's not just solving problems, but it is a creative source of, almost, adventure, and that's where creativity and the arts are so important to this process.

RW That's where you have to introduce the notion of *joy* into the fundamentals of human distinctiveness. I remember reading a government paper on educational strategy a couple of years ago, and, after wading through a few indigestible and boring pages, thinking gloomily that nobody would ever deduce from this that learning made you happy.

MZ That's the other thing that's recurring throughout our conversations, too, is the training of imagination, and also that learning is part of our evolution, in that sense – and the learning comes through imagination and creativity, joy and wonder.

RW It's not just a humanities thing. The scientist will regularly say there is joy involved in the process they're involved in.

MZ If they allow it. If we all allow it, I mean. It's not just discipline specific. This is where the work on mystery and imagination that we've been exploring is part of the way of grasping how meaningful acts do come to life in many ways through literature, or through art.

RW I guess the evolutionary biologist would say, 'Well, evolution has mysteriously come up with internal, "organic" rewards for certain kinds of behaviour, in that we feel happy when we do certain things.' Fair enough, but how very 'clever' of evolution! Why should we need the motivating joy? Do we programme into machines a sense of satisfaction with what they do so they'll do it well? No, we don't; I don't know what a joyful machine would look like.

MZ Well, that would be interesting – what would a joyful machine look like?!

RW I hand that over to the AI experts. But even if we want to talk reductively about the release of endorphin as a reward for certain kinds of behaviour, I'd add the question, 'Why do we flourish *in* and *with* the sort of system where an active sense of joy, an active sense of presence, wonder, participation, makes our actions both more satisfying and more effective?'

MZ That's something we can't answer, in some ways, yet other 'discourses of faith' also address these kinds of realities . . .

RW If you put it in the context of a sort of overarching activity or energy in which (to borrow the traditional Indian terminology) being, intelligence and bliss all belong together, then you begin to see why it might make sense. I think that kind of convergence about the nature of the overarching environment of our existence is a feature of pretty well every major religious tradition.

However exactly it's expressed, there is that fundamental recognition of a comprehensive, active reality in which we live, which can be characterised as real, as intelligent, and as reflexively joyful or self-contemplating – from Aristotle's 'contemplation of contemplation', *noeseos noesis*, to the Hindu Sacchidananda (being, intelligence and bliss) to Thomas Aquinas explaining the Trinity in terms of God's awareness of and delight in God's self. In other words, we're made not only to see, but to enjoy, to behold and to participate; to be transformed by what we see.

MZ   Yes, and being transformed by what we encounter involves an openness or gratitude toward others, and to different world views. I think that part of the beholder and the transformation, then, is where we go awry.

RW   Yes.

MZ   We don't seem to understand that relation. And I'm wondering, again, how this experience is very practical, too, being transformed by what we see, or being able to encounter a difference ... When I was coming here, there was a woman and her son on the train. Her son, a young man, had some kind of cerebral palsy. They sat in the train facing me and he was boisterous and engaged with the life around him, and I started thinking, 'Why is it that we always consider that somebody else has the disability?'

RW   It is a very interesting point. I think in that particular area where 'disability' is concerned, we are in danger of losing the plot these days, by setting up a sort of standardised humanity, to which people really ought to conform, because anything else is such a problem. A friend of mine, a very well-known theologian, has a son, now an adult, who has had immensely complex learning difficulties for most of his life. What my friend said was that she had learned, in looking after him, that *she* was the one who had 'learning disabilities'; she had the struggle to assimilate and adapt to and imagine this very different life that was also so intimately part of her own—

MZ   Yes. This is the issue, and this what I felt so starkly with this young man—

RW   She had to learn his language.

MZ   It comes back to meaningful acts and response and recognition. It's more a question, 'What do I have to learn here?', rather than it being annoyance that my feet can't fit in the carriage ... or whatever the change in 'our' perception needs to be. And it's something to do with a form of justice, not so much in that cold fact sense of the word, but a sense of that attention and awareness that then allows a certain possibility of joy in the interaction.

RW   I've written a little bit about this, but my friend Phoebe Caldwell, in her work on autism, has explored this. There is a video of her working with a young man with severe autism spectrum symptoms that shows her simply listening and looking for his own 'rhythms', his distinctive patterns of behaviour and communication, and then very tentatively offering a kind of responsive echo, a response which is 'apt' or appropriate to him, to go back to the language we were using earlier. At the end of the video – it compresses what I gather was a couple of days' work – you see this young man smiling; the recognition has produced joy.[1]

MZ   This was my experience of the mother and her son on the train. They had a good thing happening, and he seemed happy. There was a real joy in their interaction, because she'd found a way to communicate.

There was a genuine love there. And it is how meaningful acts relate very much to awareness and attention, and how to move outside of your own field of vision and reality. Which connects to discourses of faith, and in the secular sense, it's about trying to cultivate those different habits.

Last time we spoke you mentioned a book that you had been reading about the habits of the muskrat. Do you remember that? It was the story about a journalist who goes to record the effects of conflicts in urban and rural life, etc., but the guy he interviews keeps telling him about muskrats and their habits. And I do think we're not paying enough attention to the things that really matter, and as a consequence and paradoxically so, the world becomes overwhelming and difficult.

RW   I think that has a little to do with something we've touched on before, which is our sense of the passage of time; and this touches, again, on the notion of scarcity and abundance. We think and behave as though time were a commodity that is in short supply. I have to squeeze it for all it's worth, 'squeeze my assets'. So the slow absorption involved in learning the pattern, the rhythm, of someone or something doesn't look terribly attractive to us.

MZ   Everything takes time. Learning takes time.

RW   Learning takes time. Yes. You can't learn the cello in four weeks.

MZ   You can't learn to live in four weeks. Life is an ongoing journey that does require imagination and skill and training. Coming back to aspects of imagination and art, I came to Marilynne Robinson's book *Gilead* for the first time recently,[2] and I'm struck by how her writing captures the notion of abundance and the passage of time. I saw a panel that you and her were on together recently and she said something about not being so keen on Flannery O'Connor.

RW   Yes, the one great thing we can disagree about!

MZ   I can see why, because Robinson is into moments of real tenderness; there's a tenderness in the carving of words and in the awareness of the gratitude, or whatever it is that's being communicated through her writing. And then Flannery O'Connor has this other approach, which is more discombobulating. I am wondering about that difference in approach to the imagination and to that sense of worldliness.

RW   To my mind, it's almost the difference between not only Marilynne Robinson or Flannery O'Connor, but also Tolstoy and Dostoevsky.

MZ   That's interesting.

RW   How do we respond 'aptly' to the complexities of the world? Well, we can, like Tolstoy, say, in effect, 'I'm going to stop you there. We are going to follow inch by inch and moment by moment how reality unfolds; you are going to stop thinking about the big cosmic thoughts and simply look at the small-scale scene, at the evolution of *this* person, how they're growing and shifting and picking up messages and making their significant mistakes and moving on.'

You are going to be pulled out of yourself, not by some great drama or shock, but by the sheer loving *beholding* of this local, slow, small-scale spectacle – which is why *War and Peace* is such a great novel.[3] It has the grand set pieces of global history, and, of course, the interspersed chapters of rather turgid philosophical reflection. But what people remember most of all is Natasha's first ball and seeing a hunt through the eyes of a dog, and Pierre talking to Platon Karatayev – these conversations and interactions where you are just entering someone's or even something's world.

That's one approach, and I think it's also close to Marilynne Robinson's way. But the Dostoevsky or Flannery O'Connor approach, in effect, says: you are so locked up in your indulgent fantasies and your self-serving picture of the world that you are going to need an immense kick in the backside to move you out of your comfort zone. You're going to need to be shocked into recognition that the world is not what you want it to be.

So let's look at the shocks of the world, at the most uncomfortable, the most disruptive, the most unassimilable bits of the world. Let's look – as in Dostoevsky's *Devils* – at somebody who watches through a crack in the door the ten-year-old child whom he has sexually abused hanging herself. Can you make sense of *that*? Or, in Flannery O'Connor's story, 'A Good Man Is Hard to Find', let's look at someone who casually kills an entire family, including a baby, in a wood one day, when the family have taken a wrong turning and accidentally met up with a group of small-time criminals. Try walking away from that with your complacency intact.

MZ   They're two very different approaches.

RW   Two very different approaches, but they're both trying to 'unpeel' us from our habitual ways of seeing.

MZ   That's about the meaningful acts, or meaningful action, and they're both about acts of faith in that way.

RW   Yes, and the very writing is an expression of faith in this sense.

MZ   At a personal level, I find with Marilynne Robinson, you can breathe, there is this beauty or pause that you encounter with her words. It's a different kind of beauty to a sense of shock and being thrown out of your ordinary habits as with Dostoevsky. In terms of justice, we've been talking about the notion of alignment and the relations between fairly seeing, beauty and aesthetics in the realm of justice.

RW   In a way, both of them are recognising that our normal ways of seeing and responding are badly aligned, or misaligned. And there are very different kinds of 'joy' or satisfaction that you get from these different writers. They are fundamentally about alignment. The challenge of the O'Connor/Dostoevsky perspective is that the way in which the radical *giving* of sacred reality moves into our lives may sometimes feel violent and even be best represented by violent stories like these. It may feel profoundly 'against the grain' because we have so inured ourselves to a comfortable world. The disruption's not for its own sake. Certainly, neither Dostoevsky nor Flannery O'Connor simply want to make our flesh creep for the sake of it. They are saying that if we really want to know how *grace* works, then in the sort of lazy, corrupt, cosily selfish world most of us inhabit or want to inhabit, this is going to knock the breath from us. And it will come as the challenge: 'Has your world view got the resources to look at this and not despair?' That's a tough question.

MZ   And it's the one we face all the time. And they all capture the potential of grace in different ways. Dostoevsky or O'Connor are telling us these truths, and we're learning something through their writing. For me, what's refreshing about Robinson is that she brings to us the potential of human action.

RW   Exactly. This is what grace feels like. Just as, in O'Connor or Dostoyevsky, the stories are about what *not* sensing or confronting grace feels like and what the cost of that is.

MZ   And there is also something about the everydayness of meaningful acts in response to people and in response to life.

RW   This is what Tolstoy and Robinson are so good at: the sense of a kind of glow suffusing the local and the ordinary.

MZ   Which we don't value most of the time, and so we lose the experience, the beauty.

RW   I've often thought that it's very significant that Tolstoy doesn't really know how to end *War and Peace*. He doesn't want to give us a sort of tying-up-the-threads at the end, but he gives us a final scene in the family life of the interconnected clans that we've got to know and love through the long story. And then it tails away with a little boy going to sleep. In one way, it's a perfect ending to the book, because it's as if Tolstoy just looks up, closes the book, and says, 'You see the point. Get on with it'. He doesn't, at this point, try to give you a great 'message'.

But poor Tolstoy: he couldn't stop himself trying to give messages at other moments in all those chapters that interrupt the narrative of *War and Peace*, where he gives you his rather half-baked reflections on metaphysics. But he knew better than that in the long run.

MZ Yes, and in our everyday interaction, often there isn't any great message. It's more about the attention and the patience, or a practical response to a situation.

RW Not so very long ago, I saw (shamefully, for the first time) Ingmar Bergman's film *Wild Strawberries*.[4] Reflecting on it, one of the most remarkable things about that film is that you're always expecting something to Happen, with a capital 'H', and it really doesn't. So that what it ends up doing is something very Tolstoyan.

MZ That's what I like about Robinson's *Gilead*, too. It's almost like nothing much really happens.

RW Nothing much really happens, no. Why should it?

MZ The ordinariness is the stuff of this life. What happens. The meaningful acts.

RW I remember when I first read Iris Murdoch's book, *The Sovereignty of Good*,[5] being struck by her account of what moral change is like; she talks about it through the example of a mother-in-law's slowly shifting perception of her daughter-in-law.

MZ Yes, that's right.

RW   It's as if Murdoch is saying, 'Well, what *happens*?' In a sense, practically nothing, in another sense, everything. The *world* changes, the world of someone's seeing and feeling.

MZ   Yes, it is a real shift in world where it's true nothing much changes, but all of the sudden, everything is aligned differently. It makes me think about power, and we were previously talking about the public sphere and the acknowledgement of the vulnerability – not only personal vulnerability, but political vulnerability – and you mentioned the idea or the need to recognise our powerlessness.

Recently, I re-read Homer's *Odyssey* and the *Iliad*, alongside Simone Weil's essay, 'The Iliad, or, the Poem of Force',[6] and through her analysis of the *Iliad* she argues that essentially nobody wins in the game of force and power.

RW   That's it: if the world is essentially about contest, the only issue is who is going to capture the right to define it? And there's a loss built into that, because if you see this as a game in which there are *only* winners and losers, where you either have power, or you don't, where there's only the drama of imprinting your will on the world, never mind the will of the other, then what you lose is the *gift* of what's strange, the gift of what you haven't got on top of, the future you haven't mastered, the person you haven't imprisoned. That's why power, in this sense, is intrinsically tragic, it carries cost.

So if you're ever in circumstances where you're called on to exercise force or power, you have to reckon in the loss; hence, the famous remark ascribed to the Duke of Wellington (which Donald MacKinnon loved to quote), when some gushing idiot said, 'How wonderful to win a victory like Waterloo.' Wellington replied: 'A victory is the most tragic thing in the world, except for a defeat' – because, I imagine, he remembered what an actual 'victorious' battlefield really looked like.

MZ That's the issue about violence, that's why there's something appealing about being able to write and reflect about grace, the actual moments in which it's possible. That's the link back to discourses of faith, and it doesn't have to be religious faith, it can be the ability to believe in the possibility of powerlessness, in a way . . .

RW Yes, though the word 'powerlessness' begs the question a bit, doesn't it? It sets it up as a binary thing, when it's really about the person who steps sideways from that binary division.

MZ Yes. That's what I had in mind.

RW As Simone Weil says, the person who steps out of the constant mirror-imaging of violence offers the potential of grace in place of the 'you hurt me, I'm going to hurt you, then you're going to hurt me again and I'm going to hurt you again' picture, or the transmitting of it all down the line, 'I've been hurt by you, so I'm going to hurt *them*.' In Weil's view, this must involve stepping right away from this compulsive reactivity, and that involves reshaping the whole question.

MZ Yes, and that's how she sees justice, too. She does discuss the issues of harm. And that when it comes to question of harm and who has the right or entitlement over whom, this is not about justice, rather is about the *cry* of the person who is actually suffering that needs to be heard, which is outside of the realm of 'right' and entitlement. This is where the questions of love and justice come together.

And although it's a different set of questions, it is something to do with why can't we hear this at national level, why can't we hear the voices? What stops these discourses of the everyday entering into more practical kinds of public engagement?

RW   It's strange, isn't it?

MZ   It is strange.

RW   We tolerate such a level of unreality in our public discourse, and it becomes more and more marked, more and more exaggerated. And I'm not just talking about the toleration of open lies, as with the White House. I mean also the tolerance of bombastic fantasy that beleaguers us in this country with our present political deadlock over Brexit. Whether or not you think we should stay in the European Union, it doesn't exactly help that Brexit is presented as an answer to all our questions, and that any qualification of this is stigmatised as a sort of treason.

MZ   It is sad. I mean, inasmuch that we do accept such unreality. And it has something to do with a deeper connecting level, and that's why I am interested in the discourses of faith, in the everyday sense of wanting meaningful interaction. Whether we realise it or not, there is some level or desire for this kind of action, but how do we translate it into politics?

RW   Yes. We do have a certain investment in meaningful action.

MZ   And it's the public discourse itself that's lost it, and I don't know why the framing has gone so bad – I don't think bad's the right word, either . . . Why is it that we can't engage in it?

RW   To repeat something I've said here and there in the last couple of years, it's really important to look at those residual areas of our lives where genuine, local decision-making happens and to invest more in those, just to learn what it's like to make decisions *together*. The further away from negotiating a decision you are, the more you can afford to talk in the unreal, absolutist way we've let ourselves get used to. The closer you are – when the other person is not going to go away and you *have* to come to some shared perspective on a challenge that you are both looking into – the more you really have to listen and to work. You have to say, 'What can I give? What can they give? How long's this going to take?'

Often in recent decades, we've undervalued that intermediate level in our social life where we do, in fact, as school governors or participants in a local forum on traffic control, or whatever, actually exercise something of this. It's part of my William Morris cooperative-socialist legacy coming through here.

MZ   Yes, I experience it when I teach. You give students, you give people the time and the space to work stuff out, and people do it. Well, not always. I mean, you do have disagreements, of course, but there's something enabling in that time and space to think – *thinking about thinking* . . .

RW   And it does have quite a bit to do with this sheer recognition that the other is not going away, that I can't wish this or that awkward bit of reality out of my way.

MZ   Which is why global witnessing, the idea of the witnessing, is so important – that the global stranger won't go away.

RW   We close our doors to migrants and it solves nothing. It doesn't even solve a short-term issue for us. Indeed, it *creates* short-term issues for us in the UK, given our dependence on migrant labour. But the fact is (cause and effect again) that we have been complacent in a world where deeply disruptive forces have been unleashed on vulnerable populations, who are destabilised, who are literally made homeless; and *that* won't stop happening just because we put our fingers in our ears and sing loudly.

MZ   I'm thinking where to end off at this point, because I was covering most of the issues I wanted to raise . . .

RW   Maybe the point to which all this is leading is trying to find a way of talking about that *so* elusive point of balance where we are able to look at what is really before us and accept it, not with passivity or resignation, but with honesty and with a sense of – perhaps we could say a generous curiosity? If this is how the world is, how do I learn to sing in tune with it and add my voice to it in a way that will change it, not destroy it, not knock it out of shape?

MZ   Without trying to own it.

RW   And that's the needle point on which we have to learn to stand – what Simone Weil called the 'just balance', which is the title of a seriously good book about her by Peter Winch.[7]

MZ   I would like to add how the potential of creativity, imagination and justice is that we can't know everything, and there's something in the mystery of all of this that I'm intrigued by.

RW   And to talk of mystery is not at all to talk of a kind of stage curtain crashing down with a message to say, 'You can't ask any more.' It's connected, rather, to the sense of a *future,* a meaningful future, in which there will always be something to surprise. In this sense, a faith in 'mystery' is very obviously future-oriented; it tells us the good news that there will always be more growing to do.

MZ   Yes, and we need a lot of faith in that mystery; and I think this *future-orientation* gives us the opportunity to live and learn in the present, as it offers us the potential to cherish what's to come ... This is real hope.

Afterword

We ended our conversations with questions about hope. 'How else could we have ended them?', we might have said. But, reading over the whole series of exchanges, one thing that emerges – not too directly, but, I think, quite steadily and clearly – is the startling fact that our hope has something to do with the fact of our existence as *bodily, time-taking* forms of life. We can't delude ourselves that we can operate as if we lived in a timeless world where we could arrive at an ideal changelessness; we can't operate as if all we needed to do was clarify ideas and arguments, or even clarify the algorithms that would control the timeless regularities governing our behaviour. We can't help looking at ourselves 'locally' – we live here, now, speaking *this* language, familiar with *this* landscape, hearing *these* stories; we have these kinds of affinities and loyalties simply because what we learn, we learn with a local accent, so to speak.

Trying to imagine a humanity that did not work in this way is effortful, to say the least; we're left with the question of what there could be in such a humanity that we'd actually recognise as human. So much of our habitual, unconscious knowledge of how to carry on a conversation or a relationship depends on our ability to pick up physical clues or cues that we have assimilated without noticing it over time. A couple of recent articles about the potential for, and limits of, increasing the use of artificial intelligence resources in diagnosing medical conditions have stressed the risks of removing such diagnosis from the longer-term: the more informal and anecdotal knowledge that a medical practitioner may have of a patient imperceptibly makes possible a more comprehensive picture in which non-medial factors play their proper part. The doctor, like the rest of us, depends on a gradually refined and educated ability to make connections in the context of a story and an interaction. Whatever strange messianic fantasies may be popular among those who call themselves transhumanists or posthumanists, about the survival of human mental capacity when its informational content has been transferred to an electronic vehicle, most of us recognise that our physical senses deliver a variety of information at different levels that cannot readily be reduced to each other.

And if we cannot fully imagine a humanity in which body and time did not feature, if we can't imagine how we would *talk* or *listen* to a non-embodied consciousness, there is, oddly enough, hope for us. We know, instinctively, something about knowing that steers us away again and again from the fiction of a final and definitive *possession* of the world we inhabit because it reminds us again and again of how what we see, know, sense and so on is an aspect of being in physical touch with a world from which we are never separate. Our ambitions are always chastened by these reminders – as with King Lear discovering in the 'pitiless storm' that he, like any other physical agent, will get wet when it rains. The bizarre myth of our self-sufficiency and our essential separateness from matter is punctured. It is an illusion we cannot indefinitely sustain.

Right at the moment, the worldwide awakening of environmental consciousness at such an unprecedented level witnesses to the growing recognition of the illusions our culture has fed us for the last few centuries; and there is hope in this reconnection with our embodied nature. But at the same time, we have a balance to discover. What if our awareness of this embodied and local basis for all our knowing left us no possibility of understanding what was not local – other kinship groups, other languages and landscapes? This presents the risk of misunderstanding our bodily nature in terms of constructing a local ecology that was somehow sealed off from others, rather than finding our way into a sense that all localisms were analogous to one another and so could speak to one another (even if to argue). Bodily location and time-taking are things we all share. The development of a universal 'reason' or a sense of universal 'rights' is not the discovery of an abstract identity that negated all our first-hand affinities and learning processes; it is the continuing (time-taking) work of constructing vehicles for exchange, bridges across the gaps, grounded in that basic analogical recognition: this person, this culture, faces the same environmental challenges as I do. I can understand what I am doing more adequately as I attend to what you are doing.

Throughout this conversation, we have come back repeatedly to words like 'attention' and 'alignment'; and this has been something to do with the struggle to avoid any idea of universal right and justice that treats all human agents primarily as abstract possessors of universally enforceable claims. We have been wrestling with how to render a genuinely non-tribal perspective in terms that do not ignore what Simone Weil called the need for roots, the sense of a grateful and intelligent *belonging*. Weil implies, in all her reflections on the key idea of attention, that it is only the particular that can truly be the object of attention; that it is only in the particular that justice is really done (think of Blake writing about goodness and justice in small particulars, and how for him, as for all good artists, doing good in small particulars is the energy and motor of artistic labour). Throughout this conversation, then, we have turned to the works of the imagination, not only the intellect as usually conceived, to help us see what 'justice' requires, and to see how very close justice stands to *love* – love understood as the sheer will or consent for the other to be what it is, and the bracketing out of the complaints of an ego that fears for its survival under these circumstances. A full-blooded justice sees that where and what and who I am is as much the proper object of that loving will or consent as any other where and what and who, and that holding all this together means letting go of the melodramatic story of rivalry and threat. In religious terms, it is our common createdness in the divine image. But – as we have seen – there are diverse experiences that chasten and educate the ego and help (or urge) it to stand away from the stories of threat and struggle. And from that 'standing away', justice arises – the justice of seeing truly as much as the justice of acting appropriately, the justice of art and even prayer as much as the justice of dealing with hurt, poverty, oppression or whatever.

I am profoundly grateful to Mary for initiating the exchanges that this book records. We have tried not only to reflect on justice and love as 'topics', but also to conduct our conversations in a just and loving way, not looking to delegitimise or silence voices that make us uncomfortable. I have absolutely no doubt that our efforts in this respect will prove as fallible as those of most others. But the enterprise has been worth trying. As the book notes, we renewed our exchanges again and again in the wake of events that had brought suffering, terror and disruption; we were conscious of speaking in the presence of so many who carried loads of pain, loss and despair that we could not imagine, and also in the presence of a rising tide of partisan absolutism in politics worldwide. As we were finalising our opening and closing thoughts in January 2020, the possibility of renewed, acute and bloody conflict in the Middle East suddenly came closer – with all the familiar implications of how such regional conflict becomes global in an instant. But what I remain grateful for is the opportunity of interrogating, together with a friend, the obstinacy of human hope, rooted in the obstinacy of our half-conscious understanding of ourselves as sharing a fragile world and a fragile physical existence. Yes, it can be hard to see and to embrace this; but yes, it can also be the crucial test of what really counts as love, the will that there *be* what is not me and not mine. Justice and reconciliation alike begin in that moment of testing.

Rowan Williams, Cambridge

January 2020

Epilogue

June 2020

Dear Rowan,

Since we've finished our book, much continues to happen in the world. There's still so much to say, and it's the subject of a whole other dialogue, but we are at a real point of reckoning, where justice and love are ever so crucial as we live through this precarious time in world history.

I think everyone on the planet has been affected in some way by the COVID-19 pandemic. It has reshaped our everyday lives, and it is of great interest to me that it is possible for governments to slow down and 'hibernate', or even redirect economies. It is reassuring to know that there is potential for governments to respond to crises to help solve some global problems, but also disturbing that nothing has been done to address different forms of crises including the global environmental challenges that have existed long before the pandemic. What we are seeing with the curtailing of freedom and rights may also have longer term effects on our communities.

Now more than ever, it feels vital that we address what it means to belong and what we value in our lives. And as we emerge out of this pandemic, we must attend to the economic, social and political costs of the crisis that have been devastating to so many people as well as the emotional costs of this changing global environment – whether it is navigating the new and different strains on people that our reconstructed 'home–work' worlds present, or the fragile mental health, the risk of abuse, or the separation of people from each other, especially for the elderly and sick.

I want to share that living alone during this period has not been easy, and that the risk of further loneliness, isolation and despair is real for many people who are not part of existing families or close-knit communities. But I have had some comfort watching the second series of Ricky Gervais's *After Life*. As you know, I'm a bit of a fan of this television series. Gervais has a knack for touching on themes close to home – themes that seem even more pertinent to me during this pandemic. In one of the episodes, the newspaper that Tony (Gervais's character) works at is to be sold, and the motley crew of staff are devastated. By all accounts, the newspaper makes no money, but it is their work at the newspaper that keeps them together as people and as a community. By chance, Tony meets the owner, Paul, and he puts it to him that the sale of the paper will destroy people's lives. Tony reminds him that the newspaper has a vital role in telling the weird and wonderful stories of local people. After some reflection and discussion, the owner decides to give the paper another year and he recognises that he doesn't really need the money or profit he'd gain from the immediate sale of his business. The interchange is illuminating not because Tony turns Paul around, but rather because there is the realisation that *other people matter*. And this is what we can share together: the responsibility toward others and ourselves which can sustain relationships and create new social bonds. It is this leap of faith and imagination that can help provide a sense of community and solidarity. It feels to me that many of us are now confronting these very stark and terrifying issues of social and economic change. And it returns to some of the fundamental concerns in our book: What are the implications of selfishly oriented or ruthless decisions on people? How might such decisions disproportionately, and prejudicially, affect different communities and populations?

What might a post COVID 19 world look like? We are facing the deeper questions of how to respond to evolving social and economic crises and how to maintain humanitarian and social conscience and a real sense of public good. For me, what continues to materialise throughout this period are the vulnerabilities and disparate effects experienced by people in local and global terms: the structural problems that are faced within communities. And not only this, I think as we have lived through this pandemic, it has contributed to our anger, to our grief, to our uncertainty. Coupled with structural inequality and racism, the potential for harm and abuse is widespread. It is here that Simone Weil's question that we've discussed in our conversations becomes even more acute: ' "Why am I being hurt?" raises quite different problems, for which the spirit of truth, justice and love is indispensable.' This question of harm is at the front and centre of the loss of human dignity and respect that is deeply rooted in the violation of civil liberties.

As Black American activist and professor Cornel West has noted in a recent interview in response to George Floyd's death in the US: 'There is need for spiritual, moral and democratic revolution.'[1] The trauma and everyday despair through which many people live is what a friend of mine in America called 'the silent menace' of racism. The protests in the US and worldwide shine a light on the change that is necessary, and it is essential that questions of *dignity* and concern for others are part of any reimagining and reconfiguring of civil life, and ways to address the violence. As Weil has also noted, and as we have discussed, nobody wins in the game of force and violence, and it resonates with Cornel West's current call for 'love warriors' to fight with love and justice for the rights and dignity of people.

To my mind, the abject fear, loneliness and isolation that underlie our social realities need to be continually addressed, as does the 'social distance' that existed long before the pandemic. What takes place now is what will follow us for decades to come, and maybe, as the political theorist Antonio Gramsci suggested, we need inventories that compile the historical and contemporary needs for revolutionary change.[2] Most certainly, we all share responsibility for reimagining how to address and examine the distance that exists between us and how to create the steps to bridge the gaps that divide us. Nothing feels more urgent than this today.

I am anxious about the future and I am also hopeful. I hope that into the future we can write more; but for the moment, I'm keen to share these thoughts with you in these dark days, and how the intrigue, wonder and dazzlement of life can re-emerge from the ashes, so to speak.

As ever, Mary

Dear Mary

As you say, our conversations have been put into a fresh context by the events of recent months and even recent weeks. The pandemic has certainly exposed the immense inequalities in our societies. In plain terms, it has made us notice *who pays most* when things are difficult; it has underlined the very different levels of safety that different communities can take for granted. More than that, it has prompted a lot of people to ask about the basis on which we reward workers in our society. We don't apparently pay people according to the degree to which they actually make dependable social life possible – by caring, nursing, collecting rubbish, teaching, driving public transport … It's become a little harder to ignore the fact that much of the work of supporting and stabilising our social world is commonly seen as (at best) routine and uninteresting and (at worst) a matter of 'low skills'.

What are we hoping for when we emerge from the present crisis measures? I'd like to think that we could imagine a society that thought harder about the skills needed to sustain life together. These would be skills of discerning the impact of decisions and whether they affected different groups fairly or proportionately; skills in conveying to our children the vision of a genuine shared good; the straightforward skills of both valuing and implementing the practical work needed to allow people to think and plan in the confidence that society would work with them to reduce risk and vulnerability. Anything but 'low' skills, surely.

But behind this lies the deeper question which this book has been trying to tackle from different angles. How do we do justice to each other? Which also means, How do we see each other whole? The terrible legacy of slavery and the continuing abuses of racism can be traced in the fact that an entire diverse population can be 'seen' as inherently alien, threatening, violent, lawless – without any sense that, by this distorted perception, they are being punished for what they have suffered, for the barbaric disruption of lives and cultures, uprooting, exploiting, humiliating and slaughtering millions. And so that disruption is enacted over and over again, by the refusal to see and to learn.

The learning that really transforms is the process by which we grow into the skills of welcoming one another. Of course it is nearly impossible, when we inherit millennia of suspicion and mutual hurt. Of course it is *not* impossible because we are at least becoming more able (more skilled) in identifying the cunning and devious ways by which inherited power sustains itself. We have as moderns acquired some skills in critique.

The trouble is that we don't seem to have acquired anything like the same skills in putting such critique to work. And this is surely due in large part to another theme of our conversations, the need for *conversion*: we have to think about our own thinking and about our own wanting differently, and we have to act out of that new and unfamiliar place. We have to be born again.

Never mind the embarrassment that hangs around that phrase: it captures what is needed. We must begin our moral planning from somewhere that isn't just the stale and sclerotic territory of our individual agendas. We have to grasp the truth that the moral life is – just as much as the life of the surgical team in an operating theatre, or of an orchestra, or of a group of mountain climbers roped together – something in which the only way in which any individual functions successfully is by serving the successful functioning of the person next to you. Start from here and racism is manifestly poisonous rubbish; unbridled consumer capitalism and the commodification of everything is the same; piecemeal and competitive responses to global challenges – whether pandemics or environmental disaster – are rubbish. And the mindset that assumes in one way or another that the life of the neighbour is the death of Me is rubbish.

I hope that in these pages we have been trying to help people identify rubbish a bit more successfully. Looking at some of our most prominent political leaders just now suggests that there is still a fair bit of work to do: our tolerance for rubbish – or perhaps just our cynical acceptance of rubbish as what politicians talk – is dangerously high. It's as if the piles of unrecyclable plastic polluting our lands and our oceans are a sort of grim metaphor for the dangers we currently run: the danger of being choked by heaps of nonsense that can't be dissolved or broken down and reabsorbed into sense and harmony.

The pandemic and all it has brought has – for a surprising number of people – given permission to imagine things differently. The challenge is not to forget this, to go on insisting on what we have learned during this period about how things could change that we have taken for granted. One of the most powerful images of this for me is how some have been celebrating the fact that they have been able to see the stars more clearly in the last few months. How utterly bizarre it is that a civilisation which knows more about astronomy than any previous generation has so much less opportunity of looking into the night sky with clarity, with delight, with wonder. I hope and pray with all my heart that we shan't forget what we have glimpsed – and that this little book might just be an aid to stargazing.

Warmest wishes

Rowan

NOTES

Prologue: Some Reflections on Justice and Love

1   William Shakespeare, *King Lear*, 4.7.83–6, Shakespeare Online, http://www.shakespeare-online.com/plays/learscenes.html

2   Simone Weil, 'Human Personality', in *Simone Weil: An Anthology*, ed. Sian Miles (London: Penguin Modern Classics, 2005), 93.

3   Weil, 'Human Personality', 83.

4   Michael Sandel, *Justice: What's the Right Thing to Do?* (New York: Farrar, Straus and Giroux, 2009).

5   *After Life*. Los Gatos: Netflix. https://www.netflix.com/au/title/80998491

6   Charles Taylor, *A Secular Age* (Cambridge: Harvard University Press, 2007).

7   See, for example, Aristotle, *Nicomachean Ethics*, trans. H. Rackham, Loeb Classical Library (Cambridge: Harvard University Press, 1926); Alasdair MacIntyre, *After Virtue: A Study in Moral Theory* (London: Bloomsbury, 1981).

8   Sandel, *Justice*.

9   Iris Murdoch, *The Sovereignty of Good* (London and New York: Routledge, 1971).

10   Murdoch, *The Sovereignty of Good*, 88.

11   Frantz Fanon, *The Wretched of the Earth*, trans. Richard Philcox (New York: Gove Press, 2004).

12   Gillo Pontecorvo, dir., *Battle of Algiers*. Algiers, Rome: Casbah Film, Igor Film, 1966.

13   Simone Weil, 'The Iliad, or, the Poem of Force', *Chicago Review* 18, no. 2 (1965): 5–30.

14   See Hannah Arendt, *The Origins of Totalitarianism* (London: Penguin, 2017).

15 See, for example, Judith Butler, *Precarious Life: The Powers of Mourning and Violence* (London and New York: Verso, 2006); and *Frames of War: When Is Life Grievable?* (New York: Verso, 2016).

16 See Emmanuel Levinas, *Ethics and Infinity: Conversations with Philippe Nemo*, trans. Richard A. Cohen (Pittsburgh: Duquesne University Press, 1995); and *Difficult Freedom: Essays on Judaism*, trans. Seán Hand (Baltimore: Johns Hopkins University Press, 1997). We will explore some of Levinas's thought on ethics and responsibility in this book.

17 Flannery O'Connor, *Mystery and Manners* (New York: Farrar, Straus and Giroux, 1970), 67.

18 Christos Tsiolkas, *Damascus* (Sydney: Allen and Unwin, 2019).

19 Elaine Scarry, *On Beauty and Being Just* (Princeton: Princeton University Press, 1999), 89.

20 Rainer Maria Rilke, *Duino Elegies*, trans. David Young (New York and London: W.W. Norton & Co., 2006).

21 Murdoch, *The Sovereignty of Good*, 89.

22 Sophocles, *Antigone*.

23 Martha Nussbaum, *Political Emotions: Why Love Matters for Justice* (Cambridge: Harvard University Press, 2013).

24 Raimond Gaita, *A Common Humanity: Thinking about Love and Truth and Justice* (London: Routledge, 2000).

25 Cited in Weil, *Simone Weil: An Anthology,* 83.

26 For some interesting discussions on ethics, justice and love, see Nicholas Wolterstorff, *Justice in Love* (Grand Rapids: Michigan William B. Eerdmans Publishing Company, 2015) and Regina Schwartz, *Loving Justice, Living Shakespeare* (Oxford: Oxford University Press, 2016).

27 Bertolt Brecht, *The Caucasian Chalk Circle*, trans. Brecht Heirs (London: Bloomsbury, [1955] 2007).

Chapter I: On Justice

1 Roland Barthes, *Camera Lucida: Reflections on Photography*, trans. Richard Howard (London: Vintage, [1980] 2000).

2 John Bossy, *Christianity in the West, 1400–1700* (Oxford and New York: Oxford University Press, 1985).

3 See *Ethics and Infinity: Conversations with Philippe Nemo*, trans. Richard A. Cohen (Pittsburgh: Duquesne University Press, 1995).

4 Iris Murdoch, *A Fairly Honourable Defeat* (London: Chatto and Windus, 1970); *An Accidental Man* (Chatto and Windus, 1971).

5 Iris Murdoch, *The Sovereignty of Good* (London and New York: Routledge, 1971).

Chapter II: Justly Looking

1 Flannery O'Connor, 'Everything That Rises Must Converge', in *Everything That Rises Must Converge: Stories* (New York: Farrar, Straus and Giroux, 1956).

2 Early theologians who lived in the Scetes desert of Egypt.

3 *Inventing Impressionism*, The National Gallery, London, 4 March–31 May 2015.

4 Fyodor Dostoevsky, *Crime and Punishment*, trans. Constance Garnett (New York: Dover Publications, [1866] 2001).

5 Fyodor Dostoevsky, *Devils*, trans. Michael R. Katz (Oxford: Oxford University Press, [1871] 1992).

6 Fyodor Dostoevsky, *The Brothers Karamazov*, trans. Richard Pevear and Larissa Volokhonsky (New York: Farrar, Straus and Giroux, [1880] 1990).

7 Iris Murdoch, *A Fairly Honourable Defeat* (London: Chatto and Windus, 1970).

8 William Shakespeare, *The Merchant of Venice*, Shakespeare Online, http://www.shakespeare-online.com/plays/merchantscenes.html

9 Shakespeare, *The Merchant of Venice*, 4.1.317.

10 A reference to Portia's line, 'The Jew shall have all justice; soft! no haste: / He shall have nothing but the penalty.' Shakespeare, *Merchant of Venice*, 4.1.23–4.

11 William Shakespeare, *King Lear*, 4.7.83–6, Shakespeare Online, http://www.shakespeare-online.com/plays/learscenes.html

12 William Shakespeare, *The Winter's Tale*, 4.3.136, Shakespeare Online, http://www.shakespeare-online.com/plays/winterscenes.html

13 Flannery O'Connor, 'A Good Man Is Hard to Find', in *A Good Man Is Hard to Find and Other Stories* (New York: Harcourt, 1955), 22.

14 Flannery O'Connor, 'The Artificial Nigger', in *A Good Man Is Hard to Find and Other Stories*, 103–32; T. S. Eliot, *Preludes*, st. 4.

15 Flannery O'Connor, *Mystery and Manners: Occasional Prose, selected and edited by Sally and Robert Fitzgerald* (New York: Farrar, Straus and Giroux, 1961).

16 Dostoevsky, *The Idiot*, trans. Richard Pevear and Larissa Volokhonsky (New York: Vintage, [1869] 2001).

17 Flannery O'Connor, *Wise Blood* (Farrar, Straus and Giroux, 1949).

18 Marilynne Robinson, *Home* (New York: Farrar, Straus and Giroux, 2008); *Gilead* (New York: Farrar, Straus and Giroux, 2004).

19 Rowan Williams, *Grace and Necessity: Reflections on Art and Love* (London: Bloomsbury, 2006).

20 Marilynne Robinson, *The Givenness of Things: Essays* (New York: Picador, 2015).

Chapter III: Reckoning

1 Hany Abu-Assad, dir., *Paradise Now*. Los Angeles, Amsterdam, Sydney, Tel Aviv, Berlin: Augustus Films, Hazazah Film & Photography, Lumen Films, Lama Films, Razor Film, 2005.

2 Christopher Morris, dir., *Four Lions*. London, Berlin: Film4, Warp Films, Wild Bunch, Optimum Releasing, 2010.

Chapter IV: Time and Attention

1 Dietrich Bonhoeffer, *Ethics* (New York: Macmillan, 1955).

2 William Shakespeare, *Macbeth* (London: Wordsworth Editions, 2005).

3   Farid ud-Din Attar, *The Conference of the Birds*, trans. Afham Darbandi and
    Dick Davis (London: Penguin Classics, 1984).

4   Emmanuel Levinas, *Entre Nous: Thinking-of-the-other*, trans. Michael B.
    Smith and Barbara Harshav (London and New York: Continuum), 103–4.

Chapter V: Witnessing

1   This quote, and variations thereof, has been variously attributed to Winston
    Churchill, Mark Twain and English Baptist preacher Charles Haddon
    Spurgeon. Its origins are unknown, though it may have come from satirist
    Jonathan Swift. Niraj Chokshi, 'That Wasn't Mark Twain: How a
    Misquotation Is Born', *New York Times*, 26 April 2017, https://www.nytimes.
    com/2017/04/26/books/famous-misquotations.html

2   *My Rembetika Blues*, dir. Mary Zournazi (Sydney: JOTZ productions, 2020).
    https://staging.documentaryaustralia.com.au/project/rembetika-blues/

3   Rowan Williams, *Christ on Trial: How the Gospel Unsettles Our Judgment*
    (Grand Rapids and Cambridge: Eerdmans, 2000); *The Tragic Imagination:
    The Literary Agenda* (Oxford: Oxford University Press, 2016).

4   See Ludwig Wittgenstein, 'Ethics, Life and Faith', in *The Wittgenstein Reader*,
    ed. Anthony Kenny, 2nd edn (Malden: Blackwell, 2006), 261: 'Nobody can
    truthfully say of himself that he is filth. Because if I do say it, though it can
    be true in a sense, this is not a truth by which I myself can be penetrated:
    otherwise I should either have to go mad or change myself.'

5   Antoine Leiris, *You Will Not Have My Hate*, trans. Sam Taylor (New York:
    Penguin, 2016).

Chapter VI: For Love and Justice

1   Regina Mara Schwartz, *Loving Justice, Living Shakespeare* (Oxford: Oxford
    University Press, 2016).

2   See Chapters 1, 2 and 3.

3   Alan Jacobs, *How to Think: A Survival Guide for a World at Odds* (New York: Currency, 2017).

4   See Chapter 5.

5   Elaine Scarry, 'Beauty and the Scholar's Duty to Justice', *Profession* (2000): 21–31.

6   William Shakespeare, *King Lear*, Shakespeare Online, http://www. shakespeare-online.com/plays/learscenes.html; William Butler Yeats, 'Easter, 1916', *Poetry Foundation*, https://www.poetryfoundation.org/poems/43289/ easter-1916; Rainer Maria Rilke, 'First Elegy', in *Duino Elegies*, trans. Leslie P. Gartner (Bloomington: AuthorHouse, 2008).

7   Maarten't Hart, 'Castle Muider', in *The Penguin Book of Dutch Short Stories*, ed. Joost Zwagerman (London: Penguin, 2016).

8   The mass shooting took place on 1 October 2017, when a gunman opened fire on concertgoers at the Route 91 Harvest country music festival on the Las Vegas Strip in Nevada, killing 58 people and wounding 422.

Chapter VII: Discourses of Faith

1   JKPVideos, 'Autism and Intensive Interaction – A New Training DVD from Phoebe Caldwell (clip)', YouTube, uploaded 18 August 2010, https://www. youtube.com/watch?v=OhnaPJw_Wh8

2   Marilynne Robinson, *Gilead* (New York: Farrar, Straus and Giroux, 2004).

3   Leo Tolstoy, *War and Peace*, trans. Richard Pevear and Larissa Volokhonsky (New York: Vintage Classics, 2007).

4   Ingmar Bergman, dir., *Wild Strawberries*. Stockholm: Svensk Filmindustri (SF Studios), 1957.

5   Iris Murdoch, *The Sovereignty of Good* (London and New York: Routledge, 1971).

6   Homer, *The Iliad*, trans. Robert Fagles (London: Penguin Classics, 1992); *The Odyssey*, trans. Robert Fagles (London: Penguin Classics, 2011); Simone Weil, 'The Iliad, or, the Poem of Force', *Chicago Review* 18, no. 2 (1965): 5–30.

7   Peter Winch, *Simone Weil: 'The Just Balance'* (Cambridge: Cambridge University Press, 1989).

Epilogue

1   Interview with Professor Cornel West. MSNBC, 'Cornel West: The Future of America Depends on How We Respond', YouTube, uploaded 2 June 2020, https://www.youtube.com/watch?v=BkYJeMwlsto.

2   Antonio Gramsci, *Prison Notebooks*, 3 vols, ed. and trans. Joseph A. Buttigieg (New York: Columbia University Press, 2011).

INDEX